T0209251

... DOWN WILL COME ROE, BABIES AND ALL

a road map for overruling Roe vs. Wade

Thomas M. Powers, JD

WESTBOW
PRESS®
A DIVISION OF THOMAS NELSON
& ZONDERVAN

WestBow Press books may be ordered through booksellers or by contacting:

WestBow Press
A Division of Thomas Nelson & Zondervan
1663 Liberty Drive
Bloomington, IN 47403
www.westbowpress.com
1 (866) 928-1240

ISBN: 978-1-9736-0720-5 (sc)
ISBN: 978-1-9736-0719-9 (hc)
ISBN: 978-1-9736-0721-2 (e)

Library of Congress Control Number: 2018900037

Print information available on the last page.

WestBow Press rev. date: 04/17/2018

CONTENTS

We have come to save the unborn
We have come to be their voice
We have come to save them from
Somebody's choice

To Dr. Joe Kincaid, The Pro Life Team, Joe Scheidler and all
those who labor long in the vineyards

HOW TO READ THIS BOOK

The first chapter touches on the history of the common law of England and its adoption by this country as regards non statutory and non constitutional matters. The next chapters chronicle how the pernicious doctrine of sociological jurisprudence and liberal politics have shaped this country's abortion laws and fatally wounded federalism itself. The chapter regarding the Tale of Two Sentences shows the unfortunate and inevitable result of the supreme court writing itself a blank check which allows it to create new rights at will.

If this book occasionally seems disjointed, it's because it's a point by point refutation of what passes for the supreme court's reasoning in these cases. For instance, the court's twelve specious reasons for inventing the right of marital privacy in *Griswold v. Connecticut* necessitate flashbacks to the historical section, and the court's meaningless meander down memory lane in *Roe v. Wade* is dealt with as it occurs. For those who wish to read these opinions the full citation to each case is given in the footnotes as each occurs. The glossary at the end of this book explains some of the terms used, and can be consulted for unfamiliar terms

I

GENESIS

A) A BRIEF AND NECESSARY HISTORY OF THE BILL OF RIGHTS

In all the years preceding the founding of the United States, the governments of the world suffered from a major, and seemingly insurmountable, defect. Kings, tyrants and parliaments could operate arbitrarily, capriciously and with no restraints other than raw power. When kings, ruling by 'divine right' were not somewhat checked by parliaments, the result was absolute and, often tyrannical, rule. This was the type of government that prevailed in England and most of Europe. These titans clashed occasionally and cooperated occasionally, but one thing was constant – the English people enjoyed few 'rights' enforceable against either king or parliament, and those were 'rights' in name only as they could be granted or denied as either saw fit.

The first thing every student of English constitutional history – including former constitutional law professor Barack Obama, Hillary Clinton and many members of congress - learns is that England has no written constitution and so the people's rights against either parliament or the king really didn't have the force of a constitution behind them. The people actually had no 'rights' that couldn't be denied at will by the House Of Lords[1] or the by the king. By the same token, new rights could be added, invented or "discovered" since there was no written constitution to prevent that either. Consequently, had the House of Lords sought to add, invent or "discover" a right of marital privacy in England, it would have been perfectly free to do so. This is in direct contrast to the American system where the United States Supreme Court lacks the power to abolish the people's rights to be free from unreasonable searches and seizures and lacks the power to add, invent, or supposedly "discover" new rights such as the so called right of marital privacy. No, wait – it already got away with doing that in *Griswold v. Connecticut*[2], didn't it?

What was needed to bring stability to the seemingly insurmountable penchant for kings and parliaments to govern by whim, fiat and *ukase*[3] so as to guarantee the rights of people was a written inviolable constitution which would clearly set forth the form of government, the role and scope of government, the rights of people and which provided for an enforcement body that would ensure that government did not exceed the powers granted to it by the people.

When the founding fathers of our country met in Philadelphia in 1787 they did so hoping to tweak and fortify the Articles of Confederation from a document which was little more than an alliance between the thirteen former British colonies as it was proving unwieldy and unworkable. Now that the king, the most troublesome player in the governmental picture, was not on board, the next greatest problem

---

[1] For instance, English law prohibiting unreasonable searches and seizures could be changed simply by overruling the cases of *Entick v. Carrington and Three Other King's Messengers* and *Wilkes v. Wood*. This function would now be performed by the English Court of Appeal rather than the House of Lords.

[2] *Griswold v. Connecticut,* 381 U.S. 479, 85 S Ct 1678, 14 L. Ed 2d 510

[3] As pointed out by Judge Robert Bork, this was the practice of the Cossacks of simply ruling by decree. He also indicated that the United States Supreme Court has pretty much adopted the Cossacks' method of ruling by decree in the area of abortion and whatever other rights the court might want to invent. Unfortunately for millions – to say nothing of the constitution itself – he was absolutely correct! This function of The House of Lords was transferred to the British Supreme Court by the Constitutional Reform Act of 2005

was establishing a legislative authority. While we had no tradition of jackbooted arbitrariness and excesses of our own to deal with on this side of the Atlantic, we also had no central legislative authority at all and recent bitter memories of what an unrestrained parliament could do. This posed the problem referred to by Mel Gibson's character in "The Patriot": "why trade one despot across the ocean for thirteen here"? [4] The problem had been largely solved when all thirteen states included bills of rights in their respective constitutions, but the problem reemerged as a much greater threat and question when a single central legislative body (i.e., the new congress) was established. This is why Patrick Henry refused to become a delegate as he "smelt a rat"[5]. Patrick Henry, of course, was right in that the delegates had absolutely no intention of having a bill of rights as part of the constitution or of restraining the new central legislative authority in any way from exceeding its twenty three specific grants of power.

In solving the problem posed by the inadequacies of the Articles of Confederation while at the same time avoiding the problems that had always been the bane of governments and the governed, the founding fathers created a document unique in the history of the world – the United States Constitution which was as widely heralded as was Lexington and Concord's 'shot heard round the world'. The United States was seen as the Shining City on the Hill – just imagine, a government devoid of a king [the death knell of the 'divine right of kings' fiction], embodying the ideals of the Declaration of Independence where it is acknowledged that governments obtain their legitimacy from the consent of the governed, and embodying the best theories of government from thinkers as diverse as Locke, Diderot, Montesquieu and Voltaire. In the words of Warren Burger, "Our constitution has had as great an impact on humanity as the splitting of the atom."[6]

It seems the constitution was honored everywhere. In 1878, William

---

[4] Historically, it was no less a patriot than Patrick Henry who posed the question of trading a foreign despot for one of our own, Drinker Bowen, *op. cit,* page 1 of forward to second edition by Chief Justice Warren Burger.

[5] Drinker Bowen, *op. cit.,* at p. 18

[6] Drinker Bowen., *op. cit.,* forward by Warren Burger, p. 2

Gladstone, four time prime minister of England, described the United States Constitution as "the most wonderful work ever struck off at a given time by the brain and purpose of man."[7] Our constitution formed the framework for the first post colonial African democracies and still forms the framework for the emerging democracies of the world; our constitution and representative form of government inspired the Arab Spring of revolts against dictators that is now taking place in Libya, Egypt and much of the Middle East. Support and esteem for this 'most wonderful work', however, has not had such an easy road in our own country despite the fact that presidents and supreme court justices take an oath to protect and defend the constitution against all enemies – foreign and domestic. American progressives like former Princeton professor and United States President Woodrow Wilson have been barely able to contain their contempt for it as the constitution was seen as an impediment to "social planners"[8]. Others, such as Roscoe Pound, progressive dean of Harvard Law School, were somewhat less open about their contempt for the constitution and for the common folk of the country – he saw himself as part of the intellectual elitist class which should naturally be in charge. Pound pretty much ignored the groundbreaking principles behind the constitution and therefore saw it as just another document that might have had some historical value, but one which should be gotten around lest it interfere with what he, Wilson and the other progressives wanted to do.[9] Wilson, like today's progressives and liberals, was a social planner and social engineer, and socialism, communism and totalitarianism were then in the air, and the constitution protected us from them. However, now that Wilson's and Pound's oxes were being gored, they were unable to

[7] Meese, Spalding and Forte, editors, The Heritage Guide to the Constitution (Washington, D.C., Regency Publishing, Inc. 2005)

[8] Actually. Wilson was partially right in that it is the constitution that has preserved our republic from social planners like him and today's progressives, from communism, socialism and mob rule, and which may yet deliver us from totalitarianism which is the natural end of progressivism.

[9] Progressives then, as now, believed in the forced perfection of man, with the progressives themselves being the role models and the government being the enforcer.

see themselves as those domestic enemies of the constitution you here so much about in oaths of office.

Pound was the founder of "sociological jurisprudence", a movement that could have had some merit if honestly applied in a country that does not have a written constitution, but is simply not appropriate for one that does. Pound and his fellow progressive jurists believed that law's purpose is to achieve social aims. Legal rules, including constitutional rights, can only be deduced from first principles.[10] Judges should therefore use "social facts" when interpreting the constitution. While this approach may sound only mildly dangerous and a good guide to legislators, judges have nothing to do with this, and changing legal rules so that the constitution itself can be changed to suit the views of a particular justice or the group in whose eyes he wants to be deemed "enlightened" is anathema to the separation of powers, our system of government and the constitution itself.[11]

Pound himself admitted that his approach would render things constitutional that in the past would have been unconstitutional and that the constitution was merely a guide. The word "progressive", whether applied to the movement itself or just to the manner of interpreting the constitution has, at first blush, a warm fuzzy and a connotation of improvement on the way to achieving a laudable goal. That's where the problem begins as many are willingly mislead by this clever naming device. "Progress" simply denotes movement – away from something and toward something else. While we may all be pleased that the construction of our dream house is progressing, we would be less than pleased to learn that the cancer has progressed to fourth stage metastatic disease. While it may be good that your son is finally showing progress in math, it's not so good that the gangrene has progressed so far that his entire leg has to be amputated. In the sense that progressives advocate (as did Wilson, Pound and as do today's

---

[10] Since our constitution is the first principle of constitutional law, there is no need to "deduce" it.

[11] This is not to say that anathema is not often followed; indeed, it is followed far too often by the supreme court.

progressives), it means moving away from the constitution and toward totalitarianism, progressivism's inevitable end.

In the old days, it was the king and parliament that the people needed protection from and who had to be restrained, but there was no written constitution or bill of rights in England that could accomplish this. In the newly formed United States, it was congress that needed to be restrained – the only difference in curbing unrestrained power was that here, for the first time in history, there WAS a written constitution with a written bill of rights that would stop the central power from over expanding its limited grant of power and from trampling the rights of the governed. This novel concept and world shaking breakthrough was as much a menace to tyrants and elitists who 'just knew best' what was good for the rest of us as it was an unequalled benchmark for the rights of the governed.

This is why the United State Constitution was hailed around the world as a breakthrough in liberty and government. This is also why it was held in contempt by such diverse persons as Woodrow Wilson who saw it as an impediment to "social planners" and Adolph Hitler who saw it as a hindrance to tyrants. Roscoe Pound was awarded a prize by the Third Reich for his work in fostering statism and undermining the constitution. History has shown that corruption by power is a vicious circle which cannot be stopped: when one group 'knows best', and has the strength to do so, it loses no time in imposing its interests, plans and programs on the rest of us if left unchecked. In time, another group will gain enough power so that it can 'know best' and force its programs and plans on the governed if not restrained from doing so. The only truly progressive idea in this whole vicious cycle has been the United States Constitution itself, the very document that the progressives are trying to undermine because they 'know best' and would like to engage in social engineering, wealth redistribution, a new world order and so on. Various minor social programs and approaches ought to be tried by the various legislative bodies as that is what elected officials are elected to do – as long as those social experiments, plans and programs are kept in check by the United States Constitution. Indeed, there is much about our country that ought not be changed at all. The constitution has so far managed to protect us from socialism, communism, national socialism, fascism and government by outright tyranny, so there's no point in throwing out the baby with the perceived bathwater.

Were it just simple elitism and narcissism we were dealing with, there would be no big problem –people with the views of Wilson and Pound have the right, under our constitution, to hold whatever opinions they wish to hold. The long term damage wrought by Roscoe Pound, however, by urging the following of the common law approach—suitable only to a series of cases and traditions — to the interpretation of a fundamental written document such as the United States Constitution has been particularly pernicious as eventually that approach renders the actual carefully chosen words of the constitution meaningless. This would leave the governed masses once again at the mercy of parliaments, social planners, socialists, progressives, one worlders and so forth. No actual progress in government would have been made since 1789 .Why, even that noted liberal scholar and historian, Barney Frank (D Mass.) sees the constitution as an ". . . obscure, inscrutable tract" and "perversely sacred text from an ancient civilization".[12]

Even back then it was greatly feared, however, that without a supreme judicial authority to guarantee against the central legislative body's anticipated penchant for overreaching its limited grant of authority there would be nothing to restrain the new congress. Those proposing the reccomendatory amendments that eventually became the bill of rights were right about this: they knew that the new congress couldn't be trusted to act on the honor system – and didn't want it to be - and that it would seek to increase its power as soon and as much as it thought it could get away with. In fact, despite establishing a supreme court in hopes of keeping congress in check, the ink was

---

[12] Remarks made by Barney Frank upon learning that the United States Constitution would be read aloud and honored in 2011 at the opening session of Congress. Of course, Barney Frank owed his very job to this obscure and inscrutable tract governing the ancient custom of affording Massachusetts representatives in congress.

barely dry on the constitution before congress began to exceed the limits of its granted authority. As I write this in 2011, the extent and scope of congressional "authority" has been steadily overreached for 222 years now with no end in sight.[13]

The constitution as originally written did not contain any significant restraints on congressional power, although the grant of its power was specific and limited in the first place. The 23 limited grants of power to congress are contained in Article I, section 8 of the constitution, covering such diverse things as building forts, punishing pirates and borrowing money. The only constitutional limits the founders were willing to put on congressional power were contained in Article 1, section 9 of the constitution. Congress was restrained in 8 areas – from suspending the writ of habeas corpus to bestowing titles of nobility. Although congress was not granted the authority to do any of these things and supposedly (on the honor system) would never dream of doing such things in the first place, only these few restrictions were felt to be important enough to actually be contained in the constitution as written by the convention at Philadelphia in 1787.

If a legislative power could not be exercised by congress, it would naturally follow that such a power could be exercised only by a state legislature. At least one of the founders – he being the draftsman— could follow this logic and so the restriction stating "The powers not delegated to the United States by the Constitution, nor prohibited by it to the States, are reserved to the States, respectively, or to the people" was originally Article Four of the first draft of the constitution. Even this mild and almost self-evident restriction was thought by the majority of the convention to be too burdensome, and so it was crossed out of the original draft, quite likely by Madison himself. The first draft is on display under glass at the National Archives: the original

---

[13] The most recent examples of this are the Usurpation of Criminal Law Act of 2009 [sometimes euphemistically called the Freedom of Choice Act or FOCA] and Obamacare of 2010 which seeks to order citizens into interstate commerce so they can be regulated if they do and jailed if they don't. Oddly enough, if a person could also be fined as well as jailed, congress is allowed to get away with even this constitutional assault because the fine could always be called a tax.

article Four (written in cursive in quill and that old fashioned brownish ink) can be read and the marks crossing it out can be seen. It was not to reappear for almost five years when the several state legislatures forced the founders to include it along with the rest of the bill of rights before the constitution could be ratified..

Since the National Archives is only a half block away from the supreme court building, you'd think some of the best and brightest law clerks, or even the occasional supreme court justice, might have taken a stroll over there during lunch hour to learn something. Despite the fact that it soon became apparent that the constitution as drafted and sent out to the states was not going to be ratified without the addition of a bill of rights, many of the framers of the constitution stubbornly clung to their original idea that the new congress should not be restrained at all, but cooler heads prevailed and new proposed amendments were entertained almost 5 years later.

At the First Federal Congress that convened in New York in March of 1792, over 200 proposed amendments were submitted for consideration and finally winnowed down by congress to the ten amendments [of the twelve submitted by Madison] that came to be known as the bill of rights. None of the proposed amendments even remotely referenced the supposed rights of marital privacy, non marital privacy or right to be let alone, even though most of all of the original states had language similar [and in most cases, identical] to what came to be the Fourth Amendment to the constitution. The main reason for this, of course, was not simply that the so called right of marital privacy was not widespread and all pervasive, but that it didn't exist at all.

Another reason was that all thirteen states had seen what happened to the Articles of Confederation when every state had veto power over actions of the confederation and knew how much worse it would be if every married couple – let alone every Tom, Dick and Harriet — were to have such veto power simply by claiming that some law 'impinged' on their right of privacy. The last two amendments accepted, the Ninth Amendment which created no new rights whatsoever as the founders certainly wanted to stop the inroads being made on congressional power and its key political trade-off, the Tenth Amendment (the former Article Four which was crossed out), which reserved to the states all powers not specifically granted to congress, were meant to finally put an end to it. The first eight amendments contained the forty two guarantees that, no matter what else congress managed to get away with, it would not would not exceed its granted powers in those specific areas mentioned[14].

All laws restrict a person's activities to some degree, many of the framers still wanted no restrictions at all, and all of the rest of the framers who were willing to accept some limitations wanted to accept as few limitations as possible. When over two hundred proposed amendments were submitted and that list was carefully winnowed down by Madison to the twelve amendments submitted to the first congress and then to the ten amendments that were to become the bill of rights, a reasonable person could only conclude that Madison and the first congress meant to do exactly what they did do – accept as few restrictions on the powers of congress as possible that would still allow the constitution to be ratified. Indeed, one could not help but think that only a fool or a supreme court justice with a political agenda could possibly believe that the framers [who weren't even involved in the process] really meant to accept all two hundred proposed amendments plus several more restrictions on the powers of congress to be named, discovered or invented later. Despite all appearances to the contrary, it's hard to imagine that there were that many fools gracing the supreme court bench the day *Griswold v. Connecticut* was decided. Surely some of them must have known something about our country's history. How, then, could they accidently have gotten it so demonstrably wrong as to think that "the right of marital privacy" was included when one hundred fifty eight[15] proposed amendments were rejected and the so called "right of marital privacy" wasn't even mentioned in any of them, in the English Bill of Rights, the Declaration of Independence, any of the thirteen states' bills of rights or in the United States Bill of Rights which was finally accepted by the First Federal Congress of 1792 ?The

---

[14] Hoffman and Albert, *op. cit,* p. vii

[15] And ten amendments encompassing 44 guarantees against congress exceeding its powers were accepted by that first congress.

answer lies in the word "accidently". Of course the *Griswold* court – yes, even Goldberg and Douglas – couldn't have "accidently" gotten it so wrong. *Griswold v. Connecticut* was intentionally and knowingly wrongly decided for political purposes. All the justices knew it at the time and they all have known it for half a century now. Some of the reasons they have failed to correct this act of political hubris and return to the constitution they swore to uphold will be discussed later.

When it became apparent that the mere tweaking of the Articles of Confederation wouldn't be adequate and that the convention should set about creating a new government and constitution, it was suggested that the new constitution be preceded by a bill of rights as most of the state's constitutions were. The founders had such little interest in curtailing the power of the new congress that this motion was referred to committee, not to be mentioned again until the convention was over and the constitution was already written[16]. As we have just seen, even the mild reservation of non-delegated rights to the states was too much of a restriction to be endured. When the final draft of the constitution was prepared, George Mason of Virginia made a motion to include a bill of rights. He said it could be done in an afternoon by simply taking the necessary provisions from the various state constitutions, most of which had bills of rights. He certainly knew what he was talking about as he himself had been the author of the Virginia Bill of Rights and the authors of many of the states' constitutions were also members of the constitutional convention. Not only that, but they and everybody else at the convention knew exactly what the provisions were, knew precisely what they meant, that they were put in to protect the <u>political</u> [17]rights of citizens <u>against</u> the various state legislatures and that they would become protections against the new congress. The motion lost unanimously by a vote of 10

---

[16] Hoffman and Albert, *The Bill of Rights Government Proscribed,* Charlottesville and London The University Press of Virginia 1997) University Press of Virginia pp. 340-343.

[17] Not 'privacy' rights as the supreme court claims. In fact, the reason for any bill of rights at all was to secure certain political protections to the citizens, such as the ability to speak and assemble freely without fear of reprisal

to 0 with two abstentions. This is something to be kept in mind when reading the various supreme court justices' spin on what the founders thought the words meant [that many of them had written themselves] and Goldberg's and Douglas' fictitious claim that the framers most definitely wanted to include all these restrictions and more in the bill of rights they were finally forced to accept five years later. If they really wanted to include all these and more, why did they vote a bill of rights down twice – the last time emphatically and unanimously?

B) THE 'RIGHTS' OF ENGLISHMEN

The American colonists well knew that the rights of Englishmen were not true rights at all since they could be withheld or changed. Nonetheless, the colonists had been willing to settle for these precarious rights up until the dreaded writs of assistance case was lost which, in the view of John Adams and James Otis, was what finally lead to the Declaration of Independence. For the revolutionary document that it turned out to be – it did establish that the government rules by the consent of the governed and was the legal basis for the shot heard 'round the world' which reverberates to this day – The Declaration was quite a conservative document, pointing out that separation was only a last resort and gave forty one very specific reasons that had prompted the colonies to separate from England. For all the transgressions and atrocities King George III and parliament were accused of, nothing at all was said about how either had violated the colonists' wives' right of marital privacy or right to be left alone, and nothing at all was said about how either maliciously prevented the use of contraceptives by the colonists' unmarried daughters, interfered with abortions or enforced the laws against sodomy. Starting with *Griswold v. Connecticut*[18] in *1965, Roe v. Wade*[19] in 1973 and *Lawrence v. Texas*[20] in 2003, the supreme court, however, has ruled that there is a right of marital privacy, to

---

[18] *Griswold v. Connecticut* 381 U.S. 479, 85 S. Ct. 1678, 14 L. Ed 2d 510 (1965)

[19] *Roe v. Wade* 410 U.S. 13, 93 S. Ct. 705, 35 L. Ed.2d 147 (1973)

[20] *Lawrence v. Texas*, 539 U.S. 558, 123 S.Ct. 2472. 539 L. Ed. 508 (2003)

have an abortion and to engage in sodomy that are fundamental rights traditionally enjoyed by the people.

The 1762 case of *Entick v. Carrington* was the first of three cases which established that Englishmen had the right to be free from unreasonable searches and seizures. Carrington was accused of openly disagreeing with the king and making his views known by means of pamphlets that he distributed. In that case, the king's messengers broke into Carrington's house to search for papers and things that would provide evidence against him in the upcoming criminal libel trial. This was unquestionably a trespass against a man's property – a man's home was his castle . *Entick v. Carrington* was a famous case in the American colonies – the cities of Camden, New Jersey and Camden, South Carolina are both named after Lord Camden of the House of Lords who decided the case and penned these famous lines:

> "The great end for which men entered into society was to secure their **property. That** right is preserved sacred and incommunicable in all instances where **it** is violated' [emphasis added]

Lord Camden goes on to make it even more unmistakably clear to anyone not on the Griswold court - that he was referring to the property right against trespass, and not to Mrs. Entick's vague and expandable right of marital privacy[21]. The reason that unreasonable searches and seizures were much more of a problem here than in England was not simply that the colonists were considered to be second class citizens who often disagreed with the king, but more importantly, because of the way the British Empire was financed. This worldwide colonial empire, still on the ascendency, was largely financed by customs on manufactured and other goods imported from England. The American colonists, having virtually no money to pay these taxes and no say whatsoever in the imposing of them, largely ignored them whenever possible The crown and parliament retaliated by means of having the

---

[21] In fact, we are not even told whether Mr. Entick was married – so much for the fictious claim of "marital privacy for family planning'.

troops simply burst into a colonial's house late at night, demand that the dazed and still sleepy colonist produce a customs receipt on the spot or suffer the consequences. The consequences included immediate payment of the customs tax, confiscation of the uncustomed goods or arrest of the homeowner.

We are used to seeing television detectives telling the suspect to open the door because they had a warrant or could go downtown and get one. Things worked somewhat the same way back in colonial days except that back then it was simply enough to disagree with the king or to be too poor to pay the exorbitant customs tax. The other big difference is in the search warrant. The fourth amendment to the United States constitution requires that the warrant particularly describe the place to be searched and the persons or things to be seized. The British troops or their forced helpers could simply search for whatever they wanted, wherever they wanted, seize whatever things or papers they wanted to and to arrest whomever they wanted. As if this wasn't outrageous enough, general warrants were handed out on application with no requirement other than a statement of suspicion that might or might not accompany such a request.

The fourth amendment now spells out the **procedure** to be followed and requires that there must be a showing of probable cause supported by oath or affirmation before a warrant will issue. If the magistrate is satisfied that probable cause has been shown, a warrant will issue particularly describing the place to be searched and the items to be seized. Although this constitutionally mandated procedure dramatically supports Lord Camden's view that a man's home is his property and castle, it says absolutely nothing about adding some special **procedural** rights regarding marital privacy, birth control pills, abortion or sodomy. Needless to say, it has nothing to do with a so called **substantive** right of marital privacy, to use birth control pills, to have an abortion, engage in sodomy or any other imagined substantive right for that matter.

As will be more fully discussed later, In order for the *Griswold v. Connecticut* court to reach its desired conclusion and adopt Planned Parenthood's political program, it first had to intentionally confuse the two distinct concepts of substance and procedure as it is well known by everyone not already on the supreme court that almost all rights are procedural in nature; Justice Douglas actually concluded his opinion by conjuring up a scenario where law enforcement violated the sanctity of the marital bedroom by searching for birth control pills and seizing them when found. Actually, if the search had violated the fourth amendment, the evidence could be thrown out pursuant to the exclusionary rule of *Mapp v. Ohio*[22], or if the search was valid, the evidence would be admitted. No further procedural protections were needed, and certainly no substantive right of marital privacy for family planning had to be invented.

The second in the trio of cases involving unreasonable searches and seizures was the 1763 English case of *Wilkes v. Wood*, also a case well known in the colonies because not only are those New Jersey and South Carolina cities named after Lord Camden, but Wilkes-Barre, Pennsylvania is named after John Wilkes, the person arrested by the king's minions for openly disagreeing with the king. This, of course, was not nominally a political trial, but rather another one of those 'criminal libel' trials. John Wilkes was a member of parliament who disagreed with King George III on a number of issues, including the way the American colonists were being mistreated. He had the audacity to inform his constituents and others of his positions and the reasons he disagreed with the king by publishing them in the forty-fifth issue of his journal, *North Britain*. This infuriated the king and so, one day while John Wilkes was on the way home from parliament, he was arrested and his papers were seized along with those of forty-nine of his friends. He sued the king's minions and his victory established the right of a person to be free in his own person from seizure (what we would call arrest).

While Wilkes' article in *North Britain # 45* insulting one of the king's speeches supporting the wider use of even more general warrants and writs of assistance did result in his arrest and Imprisonment. Over here, "Wilkes and Liberty" became a slogan that patriot leaders exploited

---

[22] *Mapp v. Ohio*. 367 U.S. 643. 81 . t. 1684, 6 L. Ed. 2d 1081 (1961).

in the service of the American cause. In New York, for example, Alexander McDougall, a leader of the Sons of Liberty, posed as an American Wilkes, and turned his own criticism of, and subsequent arrest by, the British into a theatrical triumph while his supporters used the number 45, the seditious issue of *North Britain*, as a symbol of their cause. Although they favored as much liberty as they could get—and then some—the Sons of Liberty never mentioned the 'time honored right of "marital privacy", because there was no such right and never had been. The colonists understood what was going on even if Goldberg and Douglas did not.

Parliament and the Crown were getting greedier by the day in adding one commodity on top of one another on which they could impose a customs tax, and then expanding the frequency of general warrants to search for, and, seize, uncustomed goods. There was no doubt that the colonists knew that the prohibition on unreasonable searches and seizures had nothing to do with 'marital privacy' and everything to do with revenue and property rights: After sugar and wine joined ale and beer on the list of commodities to be taxed, one wit acidly remarked:

> "Grant these and the Glutton
> Will roar out for mutton,
> Your Beef, Bread and Bacon to boot,
> He'll thrust down his Gullet,
> While the Labourer munches a Root
>
> . . . .
> Your Cellars he'll range
> Your Pantry and Grange;
> No bars can the monster restrain.[23]

Lest there be any mistake that the concept of freedom from unreasonable searches was a property concept only which also

---

[23] William Cuddihy and B. Carmon Hardy, *A Man's House Was Not His Castle: Origins Of The Fourth Amendment To The United States Constittion* The William and Mary Quarterly, 3rd Ser., Vol. 37, No. 3. (July, 1980), p.382.

extended to a person's own freedom from arbitrary arrest, the next case in the trio should clarify that. We have seen just how pernicious the general warrants were, but actually they got worse. Conducting all those late night searche-and hauling away all those confiscated goods, tools and pieces of furniture required a lot of manpower. This problem was neatly solved by the use of writs of assistance. If there were no passersby handy who could be pressed into service, the troops would simply go out and find some. James Otis, a lawyer and Boston merchant, defended several Boston merchants who were victims of this pernicious practice of pressing people into service to go out and search and confiscate uncustomed goods. Although he lost the famous *Writs of Assistance* case, his defense sparked the American Revolution. No less of an authority than John Adams said, "Then and there was the child 'Independence' born". It was use by the British troops of such writs of assistance in the execution of the equally hated general warrants that sparked the revolution and caused the authors of most of the 13 states' constitutions to include bills of rights that would prevent the central legislative authority (i.e., the respective state legislatures in that instance) from utilizing general warrants – nothing, of course, was said about the so called right of marital privacy for family planning, birth control pills, abortion or sodomy.[24]

Our bill of rights is not actually a list of 'rights' that the people have, but rather a list of forty two guarantees that congress won't be allowed to exceed its limited powers. Since congress was granted power to legislate in twenty three areas only—and surely would never dream of trying to exceed its authority—it could be argued that no further restrictions were needed.[25]While this argument is technically and academically

---

[24] Actually, something was said about sodomy. Not, however, in the states' constitutions making it a right, but in all of the states' penal codes making it a capital offense. Since the highest statement of a state's policy on the subject is its penal code, it's quite understandable that those politicians in robes might think that the commission of a capital crime was somehow a fundamental and traditional 'right'.

[25] In fact, this very argument was made in the Federalist Papers where all this was discussed; it was the view of those who naively claimed (or pretended to) that congress would never dream of exceeding its limited grant of power as well as that of those who didn't want any limits placed on congress.

correct, the former colonists knew from bitter experience that congress would immediately seek to violate its limited grant of authority and they most definitely did not want this to happen. Even now congress exceeds its powers on a fairly regular basis and is restrained from doing so by the unfortunately named bill of rights only in the forty two instances listed therein. Thus, when a law is held unconstitutional as being a violation of the first amendment right of freedom of speech, for example, what is really happening is that congress is being prevented from exceeding its authority in this area by the constitutional guarantee against the passage of laws abridging freedom of speech. The same would be true if congress were to pass a law allowing the quartering of troops in a person's house without his or her consent

This distinction between rights and limitations on congressional power to legislate, like the distinction between 'due process of law' and 'law of the land'[26], may seem at first like a minor matter, but the failure to know and observe these distinctions is what led to sloppy thinking and ultimately to the creating of a new "right of privacy" by the supreme court for political purposes. After all, since quartering of troops would, of necessity, intrude upon a colonist's privacy, other things having something to do with privacy could have been (but were not) put into the constitution as limitations on congressional power. Entry into a person's home or car without a search warrant would also, of necessity, be an intrusion on privacy. This could mean – or so goes the supreme court's thinking—that if a person had a **constitutional right** to privacy, any law that a legislature passes which infringes on this newly minted constitutional right of privacy could be struck

---

[26] This distinction eluded even James Madison who wrote the fifth amendment which prohibits congress from taking a person's property without due process of law: he thought Blackstone meant that the phrases 'due process of law' and 'law of the land' were interchangeable. They are not, but this mistake was perpetuated in the fourteenth amendment; this is one of the things that allowed the Warren court to invent a new supposed right of "marital privacy". Professor John Kaminski of the University of Wisconsin, however, argues that Madison did know the difference and deliberately substituted the more expansive phrase 'due process of law' contained in the New York state constitution for the phrase 'law of the land' contained in his own Virginia state constitution.

down if the supreme court didn't like it. Almost **every** law infringes on this newly-minted "right of privacy" to some degree, the laws against embezzlement infringe on the embezzler's right to take the money even where he and his wife had decided, in the privacy of their marital bedroom, that a little extra money would help balance the family budget. The laws establishing speed limits infringe on a person's right to drive as fast as he wants to, while the laws against reckless driving restrict his privacy right to fully enjoy the motoring experience. Consequently, the supreme court has pretty much given itself *carte blanche* strike down any state law it or the liberals don't like.

What the forty two guarantees essentially said to congress was this: "we know you can't be trusted, but whatever else you may manage to get away with, you can't get away with this!" As a further bulwark against congressional expansionism, the tenth amendment to the constitution[27] specifically allows the states or the people to retain all powers not specifically granted to congress. Never fear. Wasn't the supreme court created for the very purpose of making sure that congress did not exceed its grants of power[28]? Surely the limited grant of authority, coupled with the forty two guarantees, the reservation of ungranted power to the states and enforced by an ever-vigilant supreme court sworn to uphold the constitution of the United States would be enough to allow the State of Connecticut to pass a law against the use of artificial means of contraception and the State of Texas to pass laws against abortion and sodomy. One could reasonably – indeed, inevitably –conclude that, yes, those two duly and democratically elected state legislatures did indeed have the power to pass the laws that they did. One would be wrong. It is neither law, logic, reason nor

---

[27] Yes, this was article 4 of the first draft of the constitution which had been crossed out as being too restrictive. It has now reappeared as the tenth amendment at the insistence of the various state legislatures.

[28] After the fourteenth amendment — incorporating Madison's mistaken belief that the phrases 'due process of law' and 'law of the land' were interchangeable — was passed following the civil war, the supreme court's function expanded into also determining whether those states whose legislatures had powers not granted to congress were nonetheless limited by the forty two restrictions against congressional expansion set forth in the bill of rights.

the constitution of the United States itself which governs in this area, but rather pure liberal politics and the supreme court's repeated caving in to political pressure.

How did this all come about? We now have two generations of citizens who have grown up thinking that the Unites States constitution actually provides for a right of privacy because the institutions of marriage and non-marriage are both cornerstones of western civilization and that a preborn baby's right to remain alive is of lesser importance than this so called right of privacy because not all the physicians of ancient Athens were Pythagoreans!

Hang on to your hats, ladies and gentlemen. We are about to peer through the looking glass and journey down the rabbit hole that passes for constitutional law [29] in this area. On this amazing and mind boggling journey you will encounter a perfidious prosecutor, a prevailing party that has twice admitted it is wrong, a supreme court which admitted the factual basis for its decision in *Roe v. Wade* was wrong but stuck with it anyway, a near hallucinogenic concurring opinion by Justice Arthur Goldberg that stands as the worst legal document ever produced by the supreme court and one of the worst documents in all of American history, cowardice in high places, patently absurd rationalizations and meanderings that passed for legal reasoning committed by supreme court justices too numerous to count. Some of the background has already been covered: the fact that the common law approach is wonderful where case law is concerned but not at all suited to the interpretation of a written constitution; the fact that a bill of rights was never intended to be included in the constitution at all and was only reluctantly included when the several state legislatures insisted that the new congress be restrained; and that the various states had constitutions which already had these restrictions and more on their own legislatures so there could be no doubt about the reasons behind them nor the exact meaning of the words used and so forth, but there is far more to it than that as we will see.

---

[29] In this highly charged political area, the supreme court is quite capable of following the constitution when not swayed by its own politics and its repeated caving into political pressure.

II

FROM HERE TO ABSURDITY: A TRAGIFARCE IN FIVE ACTS

ACT I — GRISWOLD VS. CONNECTICUT: THE ROAD TO PERDITION

Many states in the country have a list of restrictive blue laws and outdated laws on the books from a previous era. These would run the gamut from not allowing stores to be open on Sunday through not allowing docking horses' tails and not using profanity in the presence of women. These may seem quaint to us, but all states have them and all state legislatures have the power and authority to pass criminal laws and to forbid such practices if they so choose –this is called passing a law. As long as the legislators are duly and democratically elected to a legislative body empowered to pass laws, we have a republican form of government[30]. The supreme court might think it silly, outrageous and even asinine that Michigan has a law against docking horses' tails, but that doesn't mean it can veto it under the guise of holding it unconstitutional. By the same token, it can't veto Connecticut's outdated law against artificial means of contraception under the

---

[30] Having a republican form of government is one of the few requirements for statehood per Section Four of Article Four of the constitution.

21

guise of holding it unconstitutional because it thinks it outrageous, oppressive or asinine — no, wait, it already got away with doing that in *Griswold v. Connecticut*, didn't it?

The Connecticut legislature, like all state legislatures in this country, was created by its state constitution and empowered by it to enact criminal laws. One such law, dating back to 1879, nearly three quarters of a century before the birth control pill was invented, made it a minor misdemeanor carrying a $100.00 fine[31] for a person to use artificial means of contraception. After the birth control pill was invented, some people felt that the statute should be repealed as it was outdated and unnecessary. The American way – and only proper way—to do this is for the legislature to repeal its own law. If a person or group feels strongly that a law should be repealed, the first step is to talk to your duly and democratically elected state legislator and ask him or her to sponsor a bill that would repeal the law, or at least vote to repeal the law if some other legislator should propose such a bill. If your little chat is unsuccessful, you could be more forthright and direct, sponsor a statewide advertising campaign urging the repeal of the law, attend caucuses and political rallies, campaign for your legislator's opponent and finally get your pet repealer bill introduced on the floor of the state legislature. If that fails ten or twelve times, you're pretty much done as this is a purely political question and the legislature has emphatically and repeatedly rejected your point of view. Your only recourse is to do more of the same until finally the state legislature accepts your political point of view, if indeed it ever does.

Almost everybody who has had so much as a high school course in civics knows this — and the Planned Parenthood League of Connecticut was no exception. That is why they did all of the things just mentioned, even going so far as to have more than thirteen separate bills introduced into the state legislature of Connecticut that would have repealed the law against artificial contraception[32]. They lost all

---

[31] And never-imposed county jail time.
[32] Connecticut General Assembly H.B. 313; H.B. 317 of 1945; H.B. 953 of 1947; H.B. 1110 of 1943; H.B. 1488 of 1951; S.B. 696 of 1951; H. B. 1452 of 1953; H.B. 1177 of 1955; H.B.572 of 1957; H.B. 3497 of 1959 are some examples.

thirteen attempts to get their pet political bills passed, but at least knew that it was a purely political issue. The Planned Parenthood League of Connecticut next turned to the courts and, by posing the question slightly differently on each occasion, tried to get the Connecticut state courts to strike down this law making the use of birth control pills the pettiest of misdemeanors, and lost the first four times on the grounds that the question of whether or not to repeal the birth control statute was purely a question for the legislature – Planned Parenthood was even lectured by the Supreme Court of Errors of Connecticut on this subject. Planned Parenthood admitted the law was against it when it lamely concluded its brief to the supreme court of Errors of Connecticut by urging the court

> "to consider whether or not in the light of the facts of this case, the current developments in medical, social and religious thought in this area, and the present conditions of Connecticut and American life, modifications of the prior opinions of this Court might not 'serve justice better' "

Consequently, by the time Estelle Griswold, executive director of the Planned Parenthood League of Connecticut, was prosecuted in the fifth in this series of attempts to bypass the Connecticut legislature and get the court to adopt its political program,[33] it was well established Connecticut law that the Supreme Court of Errors of Connecticut was not going strike down the law to or simply ignore it to satisfy Planned Parenthood's political goal of striking down this statute. The only possible way for the Connecticut prosecutor to lose the next round – and the only possible way for Planned Parenthood to win the next case—was for Planned Parenthood to co-opt the prosecutor and get him to file the only case regarding the birth control pill statute that he

---

[33] The other four before this 1964 case of *State v. Griswold*, 151 Conn. 544, 200 A.2d 479 were: *State v. Nelson*, 126 Conn. 412, 11 A.2d 856; *Tileston v. Ullman,*, 129 Conn. 84, 26 A 2d 856; *Buxton v. Ullman,*, 147 Conn. 48, 156 A.2d 508 and *Trubek v. Ullman*, 147 Conn. 633, 165 A.2d 158.

could possibly lose. That's right, this fifth case was a slam dunk for the Connecticut prosecutor had he only wanted to win it and do his sworn duty to uphold the law of the state of Connecticut. Unfortunately for the people of Connecticut, the people of the United States and for the constitution itself, the perfidious Connecticut prosecutor was a Planned Parenthood sympathizer whose ethics tank was empty and so the two of them devised a plan whereby the prosecutor would file his weakest possible case in the hopes of losing and Planned Parenthood was handed its only chance of winning. Both these supposed opponents knew that the Warren Supreme court had tilted sharply to the left and that they had political sympathizers in William O. Douglas, Earl Warren, William Brennan and Arthur Goldberg, the worst of these liberal activist judges and the one least able to restrain himself. This line up was a windfall for them and a disaster for the constitution. This is the type of thing that led Carol Towarnicky, liberal editorial writer for the Philadelphia Daily News, to admit, during the Roberts confirmation hearings, that those political activist judges had been most helpful to the liberals in the past, and then smugly pose this question: "If that side had won, would the state Legislature have pushed through a law [repealing the law against artificial means of contraception]?"[34]

The United States constitution simply does not contain **any** provision that would enable the supreme court to rule the birth control law unconstitutional because (1) the constitution reserves to the states the power to pass their own laws (2) the Connecticut constitution empowers the Connecticut state legislature to enact criminal laws which (3) include the power to pass a law making the use of artificial means of contraception a misdemeanor. This would prevent even a supreme court led by a bunch of liberal activist judges from striking down this valid law. A clever way around this problem was devised:

[34] Newspaper article by Carol Towarnicky, chief editorial writer for Philadelphia Daily News, appearing in Detroit Free Press, August 24, 2005. She doesn't understand the constitution any more than Goldberg or Barney Frank does and likes judicial activism when it favors liberal politics . Also her facts are wrong, although possibly not intentionally so.

why not bait the hook with the prosecution of a married woman[35] who received birth control information from Planned Parenthood and then also prosecute Planned Parenthood itself and the physician who prescribed the pills? If anything would entice the supreme court to invent a new right of "marital privacy" for the purpose of family planning, this would be it! The inclusion of Planned Parenthood as a soon-to-be-convicted defendant would guarantee it standing to even raise the question and would provide the necessary funding to finance the appeal to the supreme court

It was extremely important that the prosecutor prosecute a <u>married</u> woman because not even the liberals on the supreme court could invent a right of non-marital privacy out of whole cloth and claim that the institution of non-marriage was the cornerstone of Western civilization. If this were a true and honest contest, every football coach—indeed, most people of common sense— would know what should happen. If the prosecutor were even to bother to file charges, why not then choose a case with the best chance of winning rather that the only one the he could possibly lose? Of the six possible matchups, the ABSOLUTE WORST case, and the one which gave the prosecutor his best chance of losing was chosen – a married woman who got her birth control information from Planned Parenthood, her physician AND Planned Parenthood itself. The Connecticut prosecutor won't be the only office holder in this sorry saga to betray his oath of office, but he is the first and his betrayal was absolutely crucial to the success of Planned Parenthood's political program and allowed Goldberg and Douglas to strike the first blow against the constitution they were sworn to uphold.[36]

An appeal to the supreme court followed the refusal of the Connecticut court to change the law to suit Planned Parenthood's political request, and Planned Parenthood was again told that the

---

[35] Actually, three married women were chosen as the lead defendants to be prosecuted. They did not appeal after their guilty pleas, leaving only Planned Parenthood itself in the driver's seat.

[36] This is but the first of many instances in the ongoing saga of " Supreme Court vs. Constitution: we have met the enemy and he is us".

Connecticut General Assembly was the proper body to repeal or modify the birth control statute. The appeal, under the name of *Griswold v. Connecticut,* was decided by those noted liberals, William O. Douglas, Earl Warren and the new and worst kid on the block – Justice Arthur Goldberg. Goldberg was a liberal labor lawyer from Chicago whose previous claim to fame had been brokering the deal that brought about the merger of the AFL and the CIO. They were greatly assisted by four of their brethren who lacked the courage to stand up to the political pressure of the left. Goldberg had been rewarded by President Kennedy for his liberal politics and accomplishments by being appointed to the office of Secretary of Labor and then was appointed to the supreme court. Justice Goldberg yearned so much to stamp[37] his own political views on the nation that, despite having caused more political damage to the republic and to the constitution than any supreme court justice before him, he nonetheless resigned after the shortest term of any supreme court justice to accept a post as ambassador to the United Nations where he mistakenly thought he could play an even greater role in pushing his liberal politics.[38].

To know that Arthur Goldberg was the worst and most ambitious of the three main liberals is not to imply that he was incompetent as a judge when he could keep his politics and ambition in check nor that the constitution must remain static. Arthur Goldberg graduated *summa cum laude* from Northwestern University Law School. He was a very smart man who was quite capable of writing a good supreme court opinion when not blinded by politics and when able to exercise some impulse control. For instance, his opinion in *Gideon v. Wainright*[39] regarding the accused's right to counsel has become a mainstay of constitutional criminal law. Aside from the law itself,

---

[37] Or, more accurately, substitute his political views for American constitutional law.
[38] Leon Friedman and Fred L. Israel, *The Justices of The United States Supreme Court 1789-1969* (New York and London Chelsea House Publishers 1969). Friedman and Israel probably do not agree with my conclusion as they think Goldberg's chafing at the restraints imposed by his office and his desire to impose his political views on the rest of us was one of Goldberg's strengths rather than his greatest weakness.
[39] *Gideon v. Wainright, 372 U.S. 335, 83 S Ct 792, 9 L Ed 799 (1963),*

this established two things important to the understanding of the seemingly unrelated case of *Griswold v. Connecticut* that followed two years later: (1) it took away the bumbling idiot defense, for Goldberg was quite capable of understanding the constitution and writing a coherent supreme court opinion when not carried away with his liberal politics and (2) it shows that he did in fact know that for the concept of helper rights to be utilized (a) the new helper right must be more specific than the more general right actually contained in the constitution (b) that a substantive helper right can apply only to a substantive right already in the constitution whereas a procedural right already in the constitution can give rise only to a procedural helper right [procedural rights such as those found in the fourth and fifth amendments can never generate substantive helper rights] when (c) its utilization would promote and make more secure the actual original constitutional right.

Not only do we have a contrived prosecution, a point shaving prosecutor, a blatant political appeal and request to the Connecticut courts to legislate by means of modifying its prior opinion for political purposes, and a claim that Planned Parenthood's constitutional rights were violated, but we also have the same political appeal contained in Planned Parenthood's brief to the supreme court and an open invitation to a supreme court justice like Goldberg whom they just knew couldn't control himself.

Although the author of the majority opinion was William O. Douglas who shared most of Arthur Goldberg's ultra liberal views on the subject, it is the near hallucinogenic concurring opinion of Goldberg himself that stands as the single worst supreme court opinion ever written References will be to, and quotations from, this atrocity lest the reader think I am making this stuff up. After reading Goldberg, one is reminded of Schopenhauer's assessment of Hegel:

> "The height of audacity in serving up nonsense, in
> stringing together senseless and extravagant mazes

of words, such as had been previously known only in madhouses, was finally reached. . . ."[40]

There are three parts to a supreme court citation: the official report, the Supreme Court Reporter and the Lawyers' Edition. All quotations used in this book are from the Supreme Court Reporter, abbreviated, e.g., 85 S. Ct. 1688 . At page 1688 of volume 85 of the Supreme Court Reporter[41], Goldberg says that the "'entire fabric' of the Constitution and the purposes that clearly underlie its specific guarantees demonstrates that the right to marital privacy is of similar order and magnitude as the fundamental rights specifically protected". As we have seen, the underlying "fabric" and reason for the constitution was simply that the Articles of Confederation weren't working. When tweaking the Articles failed, the founders set about the practical and municipal task of creating a new government with three branches and were very concerned with the allocation of power among them, and not at all about letting the people or the several states have any power or rights at all. Congress, the central legislative branch, was envisioned to be by far the most powerful: It was only the enormous prestige of George Washington that kept the presidency from becoming an overlooked and underpowered office. The congress was to be given virtually free rein, although the constitution itself does forbid congress from suspending the writ of habeas corpus, passing bills of attainder or ex post facto laws or establishing an export tax. On the whole, however, the sense of the convention was that of James Wilson – to avoid high sounding and vague concepts and to concentrate on the task at hand. While it is true that those who came prepared to implement plan B prepared by studying the works of Locke, Voltaire, Montesquieu and so forth, the concept of individual rights as against the congress was almost nonexistent and they were certainly not the studied product of

---

[40] Paul Strathern, *Hegel in 90 Minutes* (Chicago Ivan R. Dee, Inc. 1977), p. 9. At least Hegel was being honest and not trying to justify a political conclusion he had already reached, and wasn't intentionally misinterpreting a written document.

[41] 85 S Ct 1688. All quotations used in this book are from the Supreme Court Reporter.

the great thinkers of the age, let alone the framers of the constitution who universally ignored them until forced to include a minimalist list of restrictions five years later. The only thought that the founders gave to a bill of tights was to table the suggestion once and vote against it <u>unanimously</u> when later brought up. Surely Goldberg and Douglas must have had at least a clue about this fact of constitutional history and law!

To be sure, had the constitution as originally written by the convention contained a bill of rights, Goldberg would have been somewhat less wrong in claiming that the "entire fabric of the Constitution" and the purpose that "clearly underlie its specific guarantees" demonstrate that the so called and newly minted 'right of marital privacy' is of the same order and magnitude as the restrictions that the delegates twice voted down before being forced to accept some restrictions on the power of congress. It appears that Goldberg, Douglas, *et al* are sold on the myth that the framers always had the rights of the people uppermost in their minds and plucked these rights off the tree of knowledge and wisdom that grew just outside convention hall in Philadelphia. As if James Wilson would reach up and pluck the right to petition the government for redress of grievances or Alexander Hamilton would pick one of these golden apples that would require a warrant to particularly describe the place to be searched and the things or persons to be seized. Goldberg next goes on to foist on us his invention of a bizarro bill of rights which parallels the one that is actually written down because the framers of the constitution were just chomping at the bit to accept even more restrictions on congress than the few that were forced upon them.[42] Understandably lacking constitutional authority to support this patently ridiculous claim, but needing something, he cites his own inability to understand as

---

[42] It is also well to keep in mind that the constitution was drafted by this country's political class: many had been members of the various state legislatures; some, like George Mason of Virginia had actually written their respective states' bills of rights and many of them expected to be members of the newly created Congress of the United States. Why would they yearn to put more restrictions on themselves than they were forced to when writing their own job descriptions?

authority for the cause he advocates. These words appear at page 1688 of volume 85 of the Supreme Court Reporter immediately after "the entire fabric" rumination:

> "Although the Constitution does not speak in so many words of the right of privacy in marriage, I cannot believe that it offers these fundamental rights no protection."

I told you I was not making this stuff up. Presumably, then, if Goldberg <u>could</u> have believed that there was no such thing as the supposed right of marital 'privacy' or a bizarro bill of rights, neither would exist. Surely this marks a milestone in judicial bootstraps logic! In fact, one might almost excuse Goldberg as simply lacking in knowledge and understanding were it not for the fact that the bumbling idiot defense has already been taken away and he really did understand – he simply wished that it were otherwise. While it's doubtful that Goldberg actually would have voted to include an easily expandable right of privacy – much less an entire bizarro bill of rights – had he been present at convention hall in 1787, he nevertheless liked to think so. The fact remains, however, that he was not there and did not vote for either the real bill of rights or his bizarro bill of rights. Had he been there, such a motion still would have lost by the overwhelming margin of at least 9 to 1.

The next item to consider here is Goldberg's loony notion, shared by Douglas, that the fact that something isn't there proves that it really is there because it must have been so obvious that no one bothered to write it down. Most elementary school students would be laughed out of third grade for having such an absurd belief, but not so the justices of our supreme court. The 'best and the brightest' claimed to think that one of the reasons Magna Carta was extracted from King John by the barons at sword point in 1215 was that the barons thought that the barons' wives weren't getting enough marital privacy and that that was even more important than were the other feudal rights actually mentioned in that document, despite the fact that Magna Carta did not apply to women at all.[43] The barons, let alone the common people, had few privileges and even fewer rights enforceable against the king: the yet-to-be-invented right of marital privacy for family planning was not even mentioned because it did not exist. The barons' feudal rights and privileges were now solidified into a brokered document, signed by King John and the barons, covering sixty three specific areas from independence of the church through the fee for a baron's eldest son becoming a knight to the number of bridges a town was obliged to build for the king. Nowhere was the right of marital privacy for family planning mentioned. In Goldberg's view, this meant that King John and the barons knew that one of the main reasons for the extracted Magna Carta was that the people weren't enjoying enough marital privacy, and that this was so painfully obvious that no one even bothered to mention it.

Parliament evolved into a representative assembly that had a real share of power. Parliament was coming into its own as a force to be reckoned with by the seventeenth century. The most significant exposition of political thought was not of political philosophers but of discontented soldiers in the Parliamentary army. Now that the kings' powers were on the wane, who gets to share in and direct the power that was moving to Parliament? The great issues of the day were debated in the Putney Debates[44] between the enlisted men and the officers. Nothing was even hinted at regarding a right of marital privacy for family planning, even though this was well after western civilization had started and during the time period when it was still ongoing. Goldberg's, Douglas' and Brennan's speculation about marriage being the cornerstone of western civilization is wholly absent. Surely some mention of it and the alleged "right of marital privacy" it supposedly engendered would have been made here.

Trying to give Goldberg and Douglas the benefit of the doubt by clothing them for the moment with a semblance of credibility, one

---

[43] In fact, Magna Carta only applied to 9% of the population — none of them women. Surely Goldberg must have known this

[44] Alpheus Mason and Richard Leach, *In Quest of Freedom* (Englewood Cliffs, New Jersey Prentice Hall Inc. 1959).

might charitably say that perhaps this conspicuous absence could be overlooked because the debates were between officers and enlisted men in a victorious army who had bigger fish to fry and that the right of marital privacy – all pervasive as it was –simply wasn't uppermost on their minds during this time. If that were the case, one would certainly expect this so called right of marital privacy to appear in the next significant document regarding the rights of Englishmen, the English Bill of Rights of 1689. It was to secure these rights of Englishmen to the American colonists for which the Revolutionary War was fought. The first two pages of the English Bill of Rights set forth the various crimes and nasty things that King James the Second, assisted by "divers evil counselors, judges and ministers employed by him" did: things like subverting the Protestant religion, suspending parliament's laws, improperly levying money, keeping a standing army, disarming Protestants and doing various and sundry other abominable things[45]. For all his rottenness, he wasn't accused of violating the supposedly all important and all pervasive right of marital privacy. Perhaps this was because (1) there was no such right or (2) that despite the now - dominant Protestants' hatred of James the Second, to accuse him of such egregious behavior of violating the right of marital privacy would be to heap just too much calumny on the head of one man, hated tyrant or not. Reasonable people would choose (1). Goldberg and Douglas wouldn't choose option number two either, but would simply point out that the right of marital privacy was so fundamental and all pervasive that it wasn't worth mentioning at all because even the most casual reader of the English Bill of Rights would "just know" that it was there and would also "just know" that a blackguard like James the Second must have violated it so many times that it just wasn't worth mentioning.

One of the most learned and erudite of the American Founders was James Otis, a lawyer and Boston merchant who represented the Boston merchants in the famous *Writs of Assistance Cases* which, as John Adams noted, lit the torch of independence in the colonies. He so

---

[45] English Bill of Rights of 1689, Avalon Project of Yale Law School.

admired the English Bill of Rights of 1689 that he copied it verbatim in his famous tract *The Rights of the British Colonists Asserted and Proved*[46]. The rights listed in English Bill of Rights, and consequently, those listed in Otis' work, didn't even mention a so called right of "marital privacy". It wasn't until 1963 that Goldberg and Douglas "just knew" that such a right was there because, after all, no less an authority than Goldberg himself said that he couldn't believe that it wasn't.

The English Bill of Rights accepted William and Mary of Orange as the English sovereigns, made it a capital offense to be catholic, declared that all and singular of the rights and liberties contained therein were the true, ancient and indubitable rights and liberties of the kingdom, provided for royal succession and prohibited the crown and parliament from violating those true, ancient and indubitable rights that King James the Second stood accused of violating. Now-this would certainly have been a good time to mention the true, ancient and indubitable right of marital privacy; no doubt it would have been mentioned if only it had existed. Goldberg and Douglas would have us believe that the reason the 'right of marital privacy' wasn't mentioned and preserved like the other rights were was simply because the right of marital privacy was so ancient, well established[47] and all pervasive that there was no point in wasting words on it and actually making it law.

In his famous and definitive *Commentaries On The Laws of England,* William Blackstone doesn't even mention the so called right of marital privacy. Sir Edmund Coke, regarded by the colonists as having the last word on what the common law of England consisted of, doesn't even mention the yet-to-be-invented right of marital privacy in his seminal *Pleas of The Crown*. No doubt this is further 'proof' that such a right existed. Pollack and Maitland's definitive history of England likewise makes no mention of this. Now, honestly, would the authors of a history book, the purpose of which was to detail for the general reader and for posterity those things that actually did exist, intentionally fail to even mention a so called right of marital privacy because people

---

[46] Hoffman and Albert, *op. cit.,* p. 13.

[47] I suppose that if "well established" really means "never having been mentioned or having existed before", those worthies might have been onto something.

reading the book to learn something would somehow already "just know" that such a right existed?

After eighty seven more years of having kings and parliaments deny the rights of Englishmen to them, the American colonists took a page from the British's book and issued their own Declaration of Independence. This wonderful document established that government derives its just powers from the consent of the governed and documented forty one different specific ways that parliament and King George III had deprived the American colonists of their self evident rights. The rights so transgressed by this tyrant, unfit to be the ruler of a free people, ran the gamut from taxation without representation to hiring Indians and mercenaries to finish the killings that the British had started.

Now would have been the perfect time to have mentioned George III's violation of the colonists' right of marital privacy if there only there had been one. Perhaps it was even more self - evident than were the rights to life, liberty and the pursuit of happiness[48] and was so important and well known and all pervasive that it was simply taken for granted that all the world[49] would "just know" that such an important right existed and would also "just know" that parliament and such a tyrant as mad King George must have violated it repeatedly, even though most of the world was unfamiliar with what rights Englishman may or may not have, didn't know if they extended to the colonists and if so, didn't know if they had been denied.

Having seen that the of the so called right of marital privacy was just as nonexistent on this side of the Atlantic as it had been in England since before the Roman occupation, the next question

---

[48] Referred to in many other previous and contemporary documents as the right to life, liberty and property.

[49] One of the purposes of publishing the Declaration of Independence was that " a decent respect for the opinions of mankind" which "require[d] that they should declare the causes which impel them to the separation.". Now, apparently, all the nations of the world—most all of whom were unfamiliar with the law or history of England—were somehow supposed to "just know" that the right of marital privacy was all pervasive and so basic that it wasn't worth mentioning?

would be whether the framers of the constitution – during the brief 14 year period between the Declaration of Independence and the state ratifying conventions of 1787 through 1789 – had discovered or fostered such a new right? Unlikely as it seemed that there could be any support for Goldberg and Douglas's wild conjecture regarding the right of marital privacy, there was always a ghost of a chance that there might be some little thing that could link their views to reality. Even though neither Goldberg, Douglas nor their "best and brightest" law clerks had bothered to inform themselves about the constitutional history of England, read the history of the colonies or of the post colonial period, let alone the history of the bill of rights[50], it seemed like the only logical and correct thing to do, and so I drove to the Library of Virginia in Richmond, the Boston Public Library in Boston, the Rhode Island Supreme Court in Pawtucket and the Pennsylvania State Library in Harrisburg to see if perchance Goldberg and Douglas had guessed right. Not surprisingly, they both had guessed wrong and there was absolutely no support for their conjecture that there was such a thing as a marital right of privacy, right to have an abortion or right to commit sodomy.

The Library of Virginia research showed, not surprisingly, that no case reported in the Confederation period, and no case in Bushrod Washington's Virginia reports through 1790 even discussed this language as it was so well known as to need no interpretation. There was nothing at Pawtucket since Rhode Island did not have a supreme court until the twentieth century. At the Boston Public Library, Dean's American Digest showed no Massachusetts case regarding Massachusetts' unreasonable search and seizure provision through 1799. It was only at the State Library of Pennsylvania in Harrisburg that any case at all was found: the 1796 case of *The Grand Sachem* which involved the question of what constitutes probable cause for a belligerent privateer to seize a neutral vessel as a prize. While privateers

---

[50] To their former law clerks who might now claim that they did so inform themselves and their bosses about this I say, "Better to be remain silent and be thought a poor researcher than to claim otherwise and admit to misrepresenting the facts, the history and the law."

seizing vessels under letters of marque are no longer common, the question of what set of facts constitute sufficient probable cause for the issuance of a search warrant for the seizure of **property** have always been – and continue to be—the sole concern of the Fourth Amendment.

It was George Mason of Virginia, author of the constitution of Virginia and delegate to the 1787 convention in Philadelphia whose motion to include a bill of rights in the United States Constitution was unanimously defeated. Since he wrote the constitution of Virginia which embodied many of the restrictions on its legislature and knew that the rest of the restrictions that the states would eventually force the first congress to include as amendments to the constitution had already been part of the constitutions of Virginia, Pennsylvania, Massachusetts and Rhode Island, he was absolutely right in saying that such a bill of rights could be written in a single afternoon simply by taking its provisions from the various state constitutions. The first order of business of the Virginia constitutional convention had been to draft a declaration of rights. George Mason, its principal author, was praised by Hugh Blair Grigsby as having brilliantly come up with a sterling document which expressed these thoughts with " a distinctness and with a severe simplicity intelligible alike by the young and the old, by the unlettered and the wise[51]."

When dealing with the elemental principles which lie at the foundation of society, Mason says nothing at all about the alleged foundational right of "marital privacy", let alone Justice Brennan's later and even more farfetched conjecture that the institution of non-marriage also forms the cornerstone of Western civilization, and therefore the right of marital privacy should also be enjoyed by people who are not, in fact, married because there is no substantial difference between the two.[52]

---

[51] John Dinan, *The Virginia State Constitution, a Reference Guide* (Westport, Connecticut and London), C. Alan Tarr, Series Editor 2003

[52] Of course, Brennan got around this part of the problem by simply lying about the whole thing. He deceitfully said that *Griswold* established the right of **individual** privacy. That will be dealt with later.

While we may be talking about the exact straightforward words of the Virginia Bill of Rights that the young, the old, the unlettered and the wise alike here who could not possibly fail to understand, apparently neither Mason nor Hugh Blair Grigsby counted on the determined liberal politics of seven supposedly neutral judges who strove mightily to misunderstand them so as to support their claim that the words really meant that it was also the rights of marital and non-marital privacy that were being protected.

As if there could be any doubt remaining that Goldberg and Douglas knew they were wrong but simply sought to impose their political wills on the rest of us anyway, some light is shed on this by Leonard W. Levy, Pulitzer Prize historian and Andrew W. Mellon All Claremont Professor of History and Humanities, Emeritus, Claremont Graduate School. Professor Levy has written or edited thirty-seven books, the latest before this article was published in *Political Science Quarterly* being *Origins of the Bill of Rights* [53]. He writes:

> "Before the American revolution, the right to be secure against unreasonable searches and seizures had slight legal existence. British policies assaulted the privacy of **dwellings** and **places of business**, particularly when royal revenues were at stake.

★ ★ ★ ★ ★ ★★

The majority in *Griswold v. Connecticut* argues that Magna Carta, and later the fourth amendment, wasn't based on a property concept after all but embraced 'all the privacies of life'. Actually, William Pitt, of Pittsburgh and 'Amazing Grace' fame[54] expressed it best [and showed that Douglas and Goldberg were wrong] when he argued against

---

[53] Leonard W. Levy, *Origins of the Fourth Amendment*, Political Science Quarterly, Vol. 114. 114, No. 1. (Spring 1999) [article obtained on line at the Law Library of Virginia].

[54] Pitt was also prime minister of England and friend of William Wilberforce.

general warrants and writs of assistance in these famous words which the supreme court must have been aware of:

> "The poorest man may, in his cottage, bid defiance to all the forces of the Crown. It may be frail; its roof may shake; the wind may blow through it; the storm may enter, but the King of England may not enter; all his force dares not cross the threshold of the ruined tenement."[55]

One of the many extraordinary things that happened in 1776 was the writing of American Declaration of Independence which spurred the definition of American ideals. Then, in the midst of the Revolutionary War, Americans engaged in the most important, creative and dynamic constitutional achievements in history, among them being the 13 first written state constitutions and the first bills of rights against all branches of government. Their provisions on search and seizure are significant because they ". . . distilled the best American thinking on the subject, constituted benchmarks to show the standard by which practices should be measured, and provided models for the Fourth Amendment."[56]The *Griswold v. Connecticut* court was later to ignore the meaning of the fourth amendment as well as all the models for it and to reject the best American thinking on the subject.

Article X of the constitution of North Carolina regarding general warrants was almost identical in wording to that of the bill of rights of Virginia. It was the indiscriminate searches of places and arbitrary seizure of persons **only** that was prohibited. Article 14th of the constitution of Rhode Island says pretty much the same thing but also affirmatively states that every person has a right to be secure from all unreasonable searches and seizures of his person, his papers or his property and also twice specifically states that the general warrants which are not to be issued relate to a person's papers and property. The constitutions of Pennsylvania, Massachusetts and the other states said

---

[55] Levy, *op. cit..., p.80*
[56] Levy, *op. cit.* p. 92

the same thing as it was the property right in a person's home which prevented trespass: marital privacy for family planning had absolutely nothing to do with it .Since the word "papers", denoting an inanimate thing owned and possessed, and the word "property", also denoting inanimate things which are owned and possessed, are each mentioned three times, it would seem even harder to take Article 14th of Rhode Island's constitution to mean the prohibition's purpose was to protect "marital privacy" or the even more general "all the privacies of life". This insurmountable hurdle was nonetheless easily ignored by the political *Griswold v. Connecticut* court, determined as it was to invent the right of marital privacy so it could veto Connecticut's valid law against the use of artificial contraception.

Is it any wonder, then, that James Madison, thinking that the authors of the various state constitutions meant what they said and that the things to be protected were the person himself and his property, proposed the fourth amendment as presently worded without adding to it some vague, heretofore unknown, easily expandable and undefined phrase such as "marital privacy" when writing the framers' own future job description?

Not surprisingly, since Goldberg knew that there was no legal or constitutional support for his desired outcome, he had to invent one by trying to make Lord Camden's words in *Entick v. Carrington* mean more than they did. His misbegotten quest was amply refuted by Lord Camden when he said that:

> "The great end for which men entered into society was to secure their **property**. . . Every invasion of private **property** .. .is **trespass**.. . ." [emphasis added]

This is another flaw inside Goldberg's original flaw wherein he claimed that *Entick v. Carrington* meant that the leading cases in England from then on forbade parliament to pass laws impinging on "all the privacies of life"[57]. Since the phrase "all the privacies of life"

---

[57] The law of England did no such thing, of course, but we're indulging Goldberg's monumental "misunderstanding" here. The use of the phrase "monumental

does not appear in the fourth amendment as proposed and as ratified, and none of the state constitutions from which it was directly taken make any mention of such a novel concept, that must either mean (1) that there never was a right of marital privacy at common law in England or the colonies or (2) that, although it was so well known as to at the forefront of everybody's consciousness they all simply forgot in unison to include it or (3) Madison, knowing that almost all laws restrict some of the "privacies of life", knowing that the Articles of Confederation failed partly because the states all had veto power over whatever laws that that congress passed, knowing how much worse and chaotic it would be if everyone could simply reject a law they thought infringed too much on the their "marital privacy" or all the "privacies of life", and knowing the history of how the inclusion of even a minimalist set of restrictions on congress was twice voted down by the convention, deliberately chose not to include such a vague, expandable and undefined right in the proposed fourth amendment.

The correct answer is (1) because there was no such right nor did the colonists think that there was such a right. Indulging another of Goldberg's conjectures for the moment and assuming, for the sake of this exercise only, that there was such a right, the correct answer would then be (3). There was no way that all thirteen states, when seeking to answer the Mel Gibson question, could in unison forget to include such a basic right if in fact there had been one. George Mason was right when, just before his motion went down to unanimous defeat, he told the convention that all its secretary (i.e., James Madison himself) would have to do was to copy the bills of rights of the various states. Now, almost five years later, Madison did exactly that, but even if any state had been willing to live with such an outlandish restriction as 'all the privacies of life' the new United States Congress certainly wasn't going to.

So far Goldberg and Douglas are 0 for 4. (1) There never had been a "right of marital privacy" in the first place and the fact that that an

misunderstanding" is charitable indeed as it's pretty clear that this was but one in a series of Goldberg's steps of forcing his political views on us by subverting the constitution.

unbroken string of documents from the Magna Carta through the constitutions of the original thirteen states (2) their argument that the prohibition in that same unbroken string of documents against unreasonable searches and seizures was never meant to apply just to property despite their clear language to the contrary, but was also meant to protect against some vague and expandable "right of marital privacy" is disproven by referring to the documents themselves as well as the history of both countries (3) the even more vague phrase "all the privacies of life" is disproven for the same reasons and that it is even more vague, expandable and undefined that is its elastic companion, "the right of marital privacy" and (4) since the various state constitutions made no provision for a bizarro bill of rights to parallel the one actually written down as the various states were seeking to protect their citizens from an overzealous state legislature while still establishing a workable state government with enough power to govern and carry on the Revolutionary War they were fighting at the time, is there any point to even asking whether James Madison wanted such an unknown and unmanageable monstrosity to be part of the bill of rights when he finally was forced on the bandwagon? If the motion to include a bill of rights had been immediately passed and expansive language had been included in such a document, Goldberg and Douglas' claim of a bizarro bill of rights might be slightly less bizarre, but the fact of the matter is that the framers voted the motion down twice . The non ratifying states proposed over 200 recommendatory amendments which Madison, after first winnowing to the forty four rights contained in twelve amendments, submitted to the first congress in 1792 .Ten of these twelve proposed amendments were passed and became the bill of rights. Late comer or not, this does show Madison's integrity and also shows how reluctant the framers and first congress were to accept any limitations at all on the power of congress – they most definitely did not and never would have—accepted a vague and expansive amendment regarding marital privacy!

Since the history of the bill of rights in general and fact that no document even mentioned the so called right of marital privacy were diametrically opposed to Goldberg's and Douglas' wishes, the Griswold court was faced with the serious challenge of how best to achieve Planned Parenthood's political goal and reach the outcome it set out to reach. This was especially problematic since Planned Parenthood itself was of no help. It's true that Planned Parenthood's brief was devoted almost exclusively to the social and political arguments it specialized in, but their lawyers had no legal support for Planned Parenthood's position [58]. Although it indeed wanted the court to invent a "right of marital privacy" for its benefit, it offered the court precious little help. It was one thing for the supreme court to say what it really meant, "we agree with Planned Parenthood's political position, dislike this asinine law intensely ourselves, are greatly displeased with the Connecticut legislature and consequently are simply holding that, from this moment on we are caving in to political pressure and there will be a 'right of marital privacy' in the bill of rights" It was quite another thing to pretend that there had been such a right in England since before the Roman occupation, that even if that's not true, the fourth amendment included one, if that isn't true, then the court wished it had been, and the political protections (redubbed 'privacy protections' by the court) had penumbras surrounding the political guarantees that congress won't exceed its limited grant of powers that would still save the day for the liberals' desired outcome. Consequently, Goldberg and Douglas pretty much made the whole thing up.

Trying for a fifth strike, let's move to the court's next foolish claim. The court was understandably uneasy with the problems posed by its first four unsupportable arguments and never really settled on any amendment that supported its claim because, frankly, there isn't any. That's why the wet spaghetti approach was chosen. This was the

---

[58] This became apparent after reading Planned Parenthood's brief at the Library of Congress. The vast bulk of it was related to sociological, political and <u>religious</u> considerations (yes, religious – Planned Parenthood was making the same argument that the Supreme Court of Errors of Connecticut had quite rightly rejected as there was no law to support it). Planned Parenthood correctly guessed that the left leaning United States Supreme Court would be less sensible, more liberal and would lack the necessary courage and integrity not to fall for this pitch. At least it was a good judge of lack of character.

approach chosen by the supreme court when it so readily abandoned its proper position of neutrality and became an advocate for Planned Parenthood's political cause. Even though no amendment actually provided for a right of marital privacy, perhaps the court could back into one by misuse of penumbras or, as Dick Morris might put it, 'legal triangulation'. Most laws do impinge on a person's privacy to some degree; five of the first six amendments in the bill of rights, of grammatical necessity, also afford protection regarding areas of privacy, although their clear main purpose was to protect the people's <u>political</u> rights as against congress. The framers of the constitution were forced to guarantee that the new congress would not exceed its powers in those forty two specific areas. This, in the *Griswold* court's view, meant that they really wanted to be forced to accept more restrictions and therefore those guarantees which also smacked of privacy contained penumbras and emanations which included more than what the words said or meant. The framers could have included even more procedural restrictions regarding the type of specific warrants to be issued before a place could be searched, they could have included a man's carriage or line cabin or provided more detail on just what type of showing was necessary to establish probable cause for the issuance of a search warrant. Indeed, several million cases have been decided applying the fourth amendment to specific fact situations, and enlarging its protection to include a person's carriage and car, barn and garage. This all could have been done without the use of vague penumbras.

In fact, the doctrine of helper rights alluded to— and then ignored by — the supreme court itself would have amply assured that the protections against unreasonable searches and seizures was given its full effect while at the same time adapting the application of that amendment to modern times. For example, congress in 1792 gave nary a thought to information saved on a person's hard drive, but there has been no problem extending its protection to that stored information. There were no computers nor cell phones to be hacked in 1792, but the fourth amendment was easily adapted to these new things. The doctrine of helper rights says simply that a helper right is one that makes more secure a specific right contained in the bill of rights. If the police really questioned whether the prohibition against unreasonable searches of a man's house, papers and possessions and seizure of papers and possessions also applied to papers and possessions contained in his barn, that self evident answer could be supplied by a helper right which would allow its application to his barn because that would facilitate and make more secure the fundamental premise and protection of the amendment, that being to guarantee a person's right to be secure in his person, house, papers and effects against unreasonable searches and seizures. That's a proper way to use a helper right – remembering that there always must be an actual and more general right or guarantee actually contained in the constitution.

Justice Douglas, in his opinion in *Griswold v. Connecticut* at 85 S. Ct. 1678 at page 1780 refers to several of these helper rights. The more specific substantive right of freedom of association is derived from the more general substantive right of freedom of assembly, because to allow people to associate with one another to discuss and refine their views would facilitate and make more secure the more general right of freedom of assembly actually contained in the bill of rights. The First Amendment contains a general and substantive guarantee of freedom of speech. Although It says nothing about the more specific right of academic inquiry or right to study any particular subject in school, those are helper rights which facilitate and make more secure the right of freedom of speech actually contained in the constitution. To hold otherwise would be to allow a school to contract the spectrum of available knowledge, and that would violate the First Amendment because people need to be able to attain whatever knowledge they can if they are to be truly free to talk about it. A general and substantive right of freedom of the press is also contained in the First Amendment, although it says nothing about freedom to distribute those newspapers once you've published them. Literally, then, the government could let you publish all the newspapers you wanted to as long as you immediately burned them or let them rot in your warehouse. It was to prevent this that the helper right of freedom to distribute newspapers came about: it facilitated and made more secure the right actually contained in the bill of rights. While five of the first six amendments are primarily concerned with <u>political</u> rights (remember criminal libel trials?), they also overlap onto privacy matters. Douglas wrongfully elevates privacy matters to pride of place and uses that theme to disregard (or, as he would no doubt have put it, "transcend") the wording of the various amendments, as the overemphasized 'privacy concerns' gives him more flexibility to help him reach his desired outcome. He next says that the Third Amendment's prohibition against the quartering of troops in your house is another facet of "that privacy" which is contained in the zone, penumbra and emanations surrounding various amendments. Actually, it's not part of a facet of an emanation, penumbra or anything of the kind. The Third Amendment against the quartering of troops in your house during peacetime is a <u>political</u> right which means exactly what it says and it can stand alone. This hated practice of a central legislative authority was prohibited in all the states' bills of rights' because British troops had in fact been quartered in the colonists' homes to enforce whatever oppressive law Parliament might have passed, and the various states wanted to make sure this never happened again. When Madison was finally forced to jump on the bill of rights bandwagon, he knew exactly what the language meant and that it was not a reflection of an emanation, penumbra or zone of privacy. The states who had insisted on this language also knew what it meant when they finally ratified the constitution whose bill of rights mirrored the provisions of their own state constitutions.

Justice Goldberg goes on to say that the Fourth and Fifth Amendments were described in *Boyd v United States*[59] as protection against all government invasions of "the sanctity of a man's home and the privacies of life". That much is true, the judge in that case did erroneously describe both of the amendments that way. *Boyd* was a fairly famous case in the development of the law regarding the most litigated question concerning unreasonable searches and seizures- – just what set of facts giving rise to just what level of suspicion should be sufficient to establish 'probable cause' for the issuance of a search

---

[59] *Boyd v. United States,* 116 U.S. 616, 630, 6 S. Ct. 624, 532, 29 L Ed 746 (1886)

warrant? Never before, and few times since, has Douglas' cherry picked quotation regarding the *Boyd* court's erroneous characterization of the Fourth Amendment and the reasons the states insisted that it be included in the bill of rights, been cited for the *Boyd* court's judge's representation of its provision and purpose, although *Boyd* did establish the principle that the Fifth and Fourth Amendments should be liberally construed to effectuate <u>the purpose of the framers of the constitution only.</u> The *Boyd* court judge, and Douglas himself, even quote from Lord Camden's dicta in *Entick v. Carrington* –in the unlikely event that any legal scholar could still think that the supreme court was right, the fact that one judge's dicta quotes another judge's erroneous dicta which has nothing to do with the alleged right of marital privacy should betray the court's liberal politics and showcase one of its many errors.

All that *Boyd v. United States* actually held was that the <u>business</u> records stored on his ship couldn't be used to convict an importer of glass of failing to pay the required import tax. Consequently, what we have in *Boyd* is a case that was not really a Fourth Amendment case, which involved neither search nor seizure (though there was ample probable cause for one), a case which involved business records rather that "all the privacies of life", a judge whose own language was dicta which relied on language from another judge's dicta which was not contained in – or perhaps intentionally omitted from—thirteen state constitutions and our own bill of rights and relied on by Douglas in hopes of achieving the political outcome he had set out to reach in *Griswold v. Connecticut*.

To keep the constitution from being static and enabling its guarantees to keep up with the times while insuring that the original guarantees applied so as to effectuate their general purpose and intent, the doctrine of helper guarantees (for convenience called helper rights) was developed early in our country's history, still is useful today and would have been all that was necessary to decide the *Griswold* case. Unfortunately for the supreme court and Planned Parenthood's political goals, the legitimate use of helper rights would have required that the Connecticut statute be upheld . That is why it was given lip service by the supreme court and then promptly ignored. The first requirement of a helper right is that it must be substantive if the right actually in the constitution is substantive and procedural if the right actually in the constitution is procedural. The so called right of marital privacy fails this test because the Fifth Amendment's right that an accused not be required to testify against himself in a criminal proceeding and almost the entire Fourth Amendment are procedural whereas the alleged right of marital privacy is substantive. The second requirement of a helper right is that it be more specific than the general right actually contained in the constitution. The right of an accused, applicable only in a criminal proceeding, not to be required to testify against himself is quite specific as are the detailed requirements of a search warrant issued in compliance with the Fourth Amendment (particularly describing the place to be searched and the persons or things to be seized). Both these amendments are much more specific than is a vague, general and expandable "right of marital privacy" invented by Goldberg, Douglas and most of the Warren court. The so called right of marital privacy easily fails this test as well. Since all three tests must be met, it's now overwhelmingly clear that there is no such thing as the "right of marital privacy" unless one was invented for political purposes – no wait, one was invented for political purposes by the *Griswold* court, wasn't it?

We now come to the third requirement and reason for the concept of helper rights to exist in the first place. This specific helper right must have a purpose – to make more secure the right contained in the constitution. A vague and general right of privacy is not what gives the accused the right not to testify and so it can't possibly help him not to testify against himself. It should be kept in mind that the supreme court had just decided *Malloy v. Hogan*[60] and *Murphy v. Waterfront Commission*[61] which opened the floodgates and would soon decide *Miranda v. Arizona*[62], turning the gusher of *Malloy* and *Murphy* into a full-fledged flood. Everyone who has watched a police drama knows that Miranda warnings must be read by the police to an arrested

---

[60] *Malloy v, Hogan, 378 U. S. 1, 84 S Ct 1489, 12 L Ed 2d 653(1964)*

[61] *Murphy v. Waterfront Commission, 378 US 52, 84 S. Ct. 1594, 12 L. Ed. 2d 678 (1964)*

[62] *Miranda v. Arizona,, 384 U.S 436, 86 S Ct 1602, 16 L Ed 694 (1966).*

suspect before his confession can be admitted into evidence. No 'help' was needed to secure these protections even if the 'right of marital privacy could have offered any.

The protections of the Fourth Amendment needed no help either as its use had steadily grown as the questions of just what constitutes probable cause and to just what searches does the Amendment apply (the only issues – not the 'all the privacies of life' issue of Douglas's wishful imagination). *Mapp v. Ohio*[63], establishing the exclusionary rule — that evidence illegally seized could not be used in evidence at the accused's criminal trial—had been decided just four years before and the boom it was undergoing dwarfed even that of *Miranda*. It needed no help from a vague and general "right of marital privacy" even if such an elusive concept could have offered any.

Imagine for a moment that there was no fourth amendment protection against unreasonable searches and seizures, but only a vague general statement in the constitution to the effect that congress shall pass no law unreasonably infringing on the right of privacy. In that event, the vague general right contained in the constitution would be in dire need of help as no guidance is given – but you could almost derive the real fourth amendment from that general provision. What is the most private place? Well, perhaps a person's home would be. Since the government can't be kept out absolutely, when and under what conditions can the government enter? How about when it has a warrant specifically describing the place to be searched and the things to be seized? Should these warrants be handed out like penny candy, or should some care be taken so as not to unreasonably infringe on the general right of privacy? How about a showing of probable cause that evidence of a crime or contraband is located in the specific place to be searched? As the *Griswold* court well knew, this is the purpose of helper rights in the first place. If the constitution had contained a vague and generalized right of privacy, the specific protections of the Fourth Amendment could pretty much be logically derived from that general right. As the supreme court knows, the specific protections

[63] *Mapp v. Ohio*, 437 U.S. 643, 81 S Ct 1684, 6 L Ed 1081 ((1961).

implementing the more general right cannot be used the other way as it tried to do. The court's backwards reasoning is reduced to this: since these more specific rights could have been derived from, or supported by, a vague general right of marital privacy if only there had been one, we can pretend that that's what happened and ignore the actual language of the Fourth Amendment entirely.

Since all laws restrict the individual's privacy to some extent, all laws, then, would impinge on his or her right of privacy if there had been such a constitutional right. The framers of the constitution, despite knowing that the new congress would immediately seek to exceed its granted powers, rejected any restrictions on congress's power, and then the several state legislatures sought to guarantee that congress would not exceed its granted powers in at least the forty two areas specified in the bill of rights. The other side of that coin is that the people would have a constitutional right – not to keep congress from exceeding its limited grant of powers in all areas as that would invalidate most of what congress has done over the last two hundred years—but only in the forty two areas specified in the bill of rights. The states could have, of course, tried to forbid congress from passing laws infringing on a person's right to be "let alone", right of "marital privacy" or right to enjoy "all the privacies of life" had they had any intention of doing so, but since they didn't want congress to be so restricted, the first congress certainly wasn't going to do voluntarily limit itself from its own overreaching as it had a tough enough time swallowing the minimalist guarantees insisted on by the several states.

A word needs to be said here about the hierarchy of authority and precedential value of cases relied on by a court (in this case the supreme court). If you are arguing a case to the court, the best possible authority to have is specific wording of a constitutional provision in your favor plus a recent supreme court case interpreting that provision in your favor. Lacking that, you'd next look for a constitutional provision in your favor. Since millions of cases have been decided interpreting nearly every word of the constitution, it's unlikely that you'd find such a provision, although something might be found regarding bills of attainder, the prohibition against quartering troops in your house during peacetime or someone trying to become president before his thirty fifth birthday. The next best level of authority would be a case in your favor from one of the thirteen United States Circuit Courts of Appeal, and the next one below that would be one from any one of the many United States District courts. Since you'd want to put your best foot forward, citing each lower level of authority is pretty much an admission that there is no higher level of authority to support your position. The next lower level of authority would be an annotation contained in the Lawyers' Edition of supreme court opinions. Next would be a decision of a respected (or in this case, left leaning) state court.

It's only when you have no judicial authority or precedent to support your position that you'd rely on a law review article[64]. Without using Time Magazine as a source, it's hard to imagine a greater admission of lack of authority for your position than to rely on a law review article. Yet that's what the court in *Griswold v. Connecticut* did, because no court – not even one from the left coast—supported Goldberg's politically-driven conjecture. That's like a physician recommending the latest Lydia Pinkham miracle cure simply because he read about it in the National Enquirer. The best and brightest law clerks, some of them perhaps history majors, may have been unable to discover the constitutional history of England or the history of our own bill of rights, but they were curiously able to locate a 1961 article from the Northwestern University Law Review which doesn't really even support Goldberg's claim. Actually it wasn't even a real law review article, but rather a commencement address given by Professor Erwin Griswold to the 1960 graduating class of Goldberg's alma mater,

---

[64] As *The Cambridge Law Journal* [58(1), March 1999, p.22] points out, the reason law review articles are of lesser rank than professional journals such as *Lancet, Scientific American* and the like is due primarily to the fact that the faculty members who supervise the student editors "... have no training and very little experience in scholarly research . . . [and because of] ignorance of most journal editors and many faculty members: professors who delegate many of their scholarly tasks and responsibilities to research assistants . . . and thus they seldom or never receive editorial assessments of their work from adults."

Northwestern University Law School. You're all probably familiar with high flown commencement addresses where the graduates are congratulated, welcomed to professional life and then urged to 'go out there and make a difference', which usually means to go out into the world and advocate for whatever views the speaker happens to have on a particular subject. This lowers its rank even further.

Professor Griswold had noted that in the 1950's there had been excessive and overzealous use of legislative committees such as the House UnAmerican Activities Committee (HUAC), and thought that the constitution should have prevented citizens from having to appear before congressional committees in the first place, let alone testify, and so referred to the dissent in *Olmstead v. United States*[65] .Despite its indignantly frothy rhetoric, all that the dissent really said was that the dissenter thought that telephone conversations recorded in real time should be treated as if they were stored records of past writings contained in books and records, and consequently a warrant must issue before such a conversation can be tapped. Not only did Professor Griswold know that the quotation in *Olmstead v. United States* was taken from a dissent and therefore **not** law, he acknowledged that the 'right to be let alone' does not exist, and agreed with later courts which upheld the convictions of several faculty members of the University of Arkansas who refused to file loyalty affidavits listing all the organizations to which they had belonged were fired, that a school teacher in Pennsylvania was fired for being incompetent when he claimed the fifth amendment right against self incrimination in similar circumstance, and that the courts in California upheld the firing of a teacher who refused to testify about alleged subversive activities. Whatever his personal views, Professor Griswold stands head and shoulders above Goldberg and Douglas when it comes to honesty and ethics. Where is Joseph Welch when you really need him? Who can forget those famous words he said to Joe McCarthy in 'Tail Gunner Joe':

---

[65] *Olmstead v. United States*, 277 US 4381, 48 S Ct 564, 72 L Ed 944 (1929).

"The people of America deserve better.
The people of Wisconsin will have better!"

As far as the caliber of the majority of supreme court justices who have disgraced that court for the last 50 years, I can only echo:

"The people of America deserve better.
But will the people of America have better if nominees who threaten to follow the constitution keep getting borked?"[66]

As discussed previously, Goldberg wasn't the first of the three main liberal activists on the *Griswold* court – merely the worst. By the same token he wasn't the first supreme court justice to revise and misrepresent the history of the bill of rights – merely the worst. The dissenter in *Olmstead v. United States* said that because the makers of the constitution knew that the significance of a man's spiritual nature, of his feelings and of his intellect transcended material things,

"they sought to protect Americans in their beliefs, their thoughts, their emotions and their sensations. They conferred, as against the government, the right to be let alone."

What absolute rubbish! The framers of the constitution did nothing of the kind. None of the 38 framers wanted to include a bill of rights at all, but were forced by the states to include one. The guarantees were for the political protection of the citizens against the anticipated legislative excess of congress – not about privacy or 'the right to be let alone'. Over

---

[66] Judge Robert Bork was nominated to be a justice on the supreme court, but when Joe Biden and Teddy Kennedy found out that he was among the vast majority of judges who knew the *Griswold v. Connecticut* and *Roe v. Wade* decisions were wrong about there being a constitutional right of privacy but was unwilling to let politics cause him to perpetuate that error, they were afraid he might follow the constitution, and so the Senate Judiciary committee refused to give their advice and consent. This has come to be known as 'borking'.

two hundred proposed amendments were suggested before being winnowed down to the twelve Madison submitted to the first federal congress, and none of them said anything about a supposed right of marital privacy or 'right to be let alone'. The majority in the *Olmstead* case held at 48 S. Ct. 568 that, "even though the Fourth and Fifth Amendments should be liberally construed to effectuate the <u>purpose of the framers of the Constitution</u> [emphasis added], ". . . that cannot justify enlargement of the language employed beyond the practical meaning of houses, papers and effects. . . Since neither Goldberg, Douglas nor Earl Warren were on the supreme court yet, who could the author of this blatantly incorrect quotation be? Was the author merely ignorant, someone who actually thought that present telephone conversations really were the same as past writings, or was he also a con man[67]? Finding out who the author of these misrepresentations was like finding out that T.S. Elliot wrote 'Cats' or discovering that Grant Wood was really a cartoonist. The road to perdition begins with a single misstep. Unlikely as it may seem, perhaps the author simply didn't know that the <u>founders themselves</u> argued <u>against</u> the very interpretation he favored and asserted as a constitutional right. Hamilton asked rhetorically and sarcastically, " And while we're at it, why not declare in the Constitution that government ought to be free, that taxes ought not to be excessive, and so on?"[68] The constitution was not to be a statement of fundamental rights, let alone a high flown and expandable one of the kind Goldberg and Douglas thought would have been a better idea. The new constitution was, in the view of James Wilson, a person second in importance and influence only to Madison himself, municipal law, positive law – what in medieval times was called *jus civile*. Not a declaration of eternal rights but a nuts and bolts document which would build a nation.

"Quite evidently, the Federal Convention looked at its work as practical, everyday, business; all along they

---

[67] His supporters would call this type of spin Brandeis' "characteristic vigor"

[68] Federalist Papers, Number 84, as quoted in Miracle At Philadelphia, p. 245

had avoided high flown phrases about the rights of man.. . ."

   When all was said and done, neither Goldberg nor Douglas actually relied on the alleged procedural "right to be let alone" anyway which they speculated that the Fourth Amendment might imply, but rather on their invented "right of marital privacy" (which – had it existed – would have had an entirely different origin according to Goldberg and Douglas theory.) Why, then, did Goldberg even bring it up in the first place? This certainly is an interesting question: the most likely answer is that even Goldberg had to give the illusion that there was some support – even by a commencement address masquerading as a law review article – for his near hallucinogenic opinion.

   The Declaration of Independence, which was also signed by James Wilson who knew the difference, is a declaration of rights. While limited in scope, the Declaration does declare that all men are created equal and are endowed by their creator with certain inalienable rights, among which are life, liberty and the pursuit of happiness. Jefferson's work, endorsed by many of the same men who later signed the constitution, went on to declare that the reason governments are instituted among men is to secure these rights, deriving their just powers from the consent of the governed. An example of a more detailed Declaration of Rights, also promulgated in 1789 for easy comparison, is the French Declaration of Rights of Man issued at the start of the more comprehensive French Revolution. There was no constitution creating a government that went along with that Declaration's high sounding phrases and that was one of the reasons the French Revolution went from revolution to reign of terror to chaos to Napoleon. The United Nations and Amnesty International have issued declarations of rights. One of the most comprehensive declarations of rights which a government never even tried to implement was that of the former Soviet Union. You'd think that a person whose job it is to interpret a constitution and an unfortunately named list of guarantees against congressional excesses in the areas listed would know the difference. The framers of the Constitution certainly knew the difference as did the signers of the Declaration of Independence, but the penumbra prone supreme court seems to have lost its way here as well. It's much easier to conjure up a penumbra of "rights" surrounding the 'privacy' "rights" supposedly contained in the first ten amendments than it is to have a 'penumbra' of <u>additional guarantees</u> against congress attempting to exercise powers that it never had in the first place.

One of the several problems with Goldberg's bizarro bill of rights was that it was homeless. Does this phantom bill of rights just hover like a shapeless cloud over the whole document, or is there a place Goldberg's fancies it might spring from? The answer is the latter, and the specific place is the Ninth Amendment which has to do with the doctrine of retained rights by providing that, "The enumeration in the Constitution of certain rights shall not be construed to deny or disparage others retained by the people." In the days before the *Griswold* court invented the right of marital privacy, this had always meant exactly what it said — that the Ninth Amendment neither creates any new constitutional rights or takes away those which exist. Precious few constitutional rights existed before the bill of rights was appended – the rights preventing congress from passing bills of attainder or ex post facto laws were two of them. There was a provision preventing the suspension of the writ of habeas corpus. Now that we had a bill of rights that failed to mention them, the Ninth Amendment said that these constitutional rights were not disparaged. Although it said nothing about elevating the millions of other retained rights to constitutional status, this is what Goldberg and Douglas would have us believe.

Among the millions of things that the people retained the right to do would be the right to play golf or practice archery, to paint a barn yellow, to play a banjo, start a multi-million dollar company or sleep on their left side rather than their right if they so chose[69] or to use

---

[69] Drinker Bowen, *op.cit.*, p. 246. Noah Webster argued against a bill of rights at all because it would be impossible to name them all, and a failure to mention them all might mean that the people could no longer do what they had always done. He used the example of a person sleeping his right side instead of his left and vice versa.

birth control pills for family planning. The Russian comedian, Yakov Smirnoff understood the doctrine of retained rights when he said, "in Soviet Union you can do nothing unless the government tells you to; in America, you can do anything until the government tells you not to. What a country!" That's it in a nutshell and that's how it had been correctly interpreted in the only three cases in our country's history before the *Griswold* case that even dealt with the Ninth Amendment[70]. While Goldberg does cite all three cases at page 1685 of the Supreme Court Reporter, it must be in hopes that no one would actually read them but, rather just accept his clever and misleading device of simply saying that the court "accepted" one of the plaintiffs contentions that the case involved the Ninth and Tenth Amendments and political rights to mean that the court agreed with him about privacy and found in favor of that plaintiff. Actually, the court **rejected** the arguments urged by those plaintiffs and by Goldberg in **all three cases!** All the court accepted was plaintiff's contention, <u>for framing the issue on appeal only</u>, that that the question of whether he retained any supposed constitutional and inviolable right to be treasurer of a political party while employed by the government involved political rights and the Ninth and Tenth Amendments [of course, this of necessity had to involve the <u>question</u> of political rights and the Ninth and Tenth Amendments].

Yakov Smirnoff was exactly right: the plaintiff could be the treasurer of a political party while employed by the government until such time as the government told him he could no longer do that. The government did tell him he could no longer do that when it passed the Hatch Act. The very purpose and terms of the Hatch Act prohibited a government employee from engaging in political activities. The court sided with the government because Mitchell had no constitutional right to be treasurer of a political party while employed by the government, and therefore could not have retained what he never had in the first place. This is not only directly contrary to Goldberg's

---

[70] *United Public Workers v. Mitchell*, 330 U.S. 75, 94-95, 67 S, Ct. 556, 566-567, 91 L. Ed. 754; *Tennessee Electric Co. v. TVA*, 306 U.S. 118, 143-144, 59 S. Ct.. 36, 372, 83 L .Ed 543; and *Ashwander v. TVA*, 297 U.S. 118, 143-144, 59 S. Ct. 466, 475, 80 L. Ed 688.

position regarding the Ninth Amendment [which he obviously had to know since he excerpted that misleading quotation][71], but is also against his entire position of a "retained constitutional right of marital privacy." In the more honest pre - Goldberg era, a person wanting to use birth control pills, commit sodomy or have an abortion would present the question thusly:

> Is this supposed constitutional and inviolable right to use artificial means of contraception retained intact by virtue of the Ninth Amendment despite the fact that the Connecticut state legislature enacted a law prohibiting such use?

A more honest and less political appellate court would then answer:

> No, an alleged constitutional right to use artificial means of contraception is not retained by virtue of the Ninth Amendment because the right to use artificial means of contraception is neither constitutional nor inviolable, but simply one among many rights retained by the people of Connecticut until 1879 when the Connecticut legislature passed a law against such use. Since the Ninth Amendment does not create any new constitutional rights, we decline your request to create one for you.

That's what the court in Goldberg's cited case of *United Public Workers v .Mitchell* would have done – in fact that's exactly what it did do as far as the Hatch Act was concerned. The other two cases which were decided against Goldberg's position, *Ashwander v. TVA* and *Tennessee Electric Power Co. v. TVA*, involved similar issues. The Tennessee Electric Power Company felt it had a retained constitutional right not to have to compete with a government built and government subsidized electric utility. Had there been such a constitutional right,

---

[71] Just another instance deception in high places.

the Tennessee Electric Power Company would have won the case as that right would not have been disparaged according to the real Ninth Amendment. The court correctly told the Tennessee Power Company that it once did have the retained right to be free from government subsidized competition until such time as the government took that right away by passing a law creating the TVA. Since the company had no **constitutional** right to operate free from such competition in the first place, the Ninth Amendment couldn't preserve what wasn't there. Since the Ninth Amendment did not create any new constitutional rights, the power company lost the case. It's hard to imagine that neither Goldberg nor Douglas knew this because, after all, there were only <u>three</u> cases, so the volume of material to be read couldn't have been that overwhelming. The *Ashwander* case was similar, but it focused on the government's power to use public money to buy the land and pay for the construction of the plant in the first place. The argument favored by Goldberg was rejected in that case also.

Pursuant to a valid grant of authority in the Connecticut constitution, the Connecticut legislature had passed a law against the use of artificial means of contraception. Although that law may have been ill advised, outdated or even "asinine"[72], the Tenth Amendment expressly reserves to the states the right to pass their own laws. To even imagine that the states which forced the founders to press for limitations on the power congress really meant that those very states themselves were the ones to be limited is to see the absurdity of Goldberg's position. To be sure, the framers of the constitution did not envision the passage of the Fourteenth Amendment after the Civil War, but that fact cannot make a reservation of rights **to** the states into a restriction **against** those very states. By the same token, rights that cannot be created against the congress don't turn into rights that can be created against the states. Nonetheless, in its eagerness to buy into Planned Parenthood's political agenda, even more mental gymnastics were engaged in by the *Griswold* court so as to make it seem that the

---

[72] In the words of Justice Potter Stewart who, despite his distaste for the Connecticut law, nonetheless voted to uphold it since the constitution did not give the supreme court the power to simply veto state laws it didn't like.

Ninth and Tenth Amendments were limitations on state power. Even if this unwarranted spin is believed, the Ninth Amendment **still** cannot be used as authority because it creates no new constitutional rights whatsoever!

As we have seen, the Ninth Amendment neither creates nor destroys rights which are of constitutional stature. Since the right to use artificial means of contraception was not of constitutional stature, how did Goldberg manage to get the Ninth Amendment appear to create such a right under the guise of "preserving" it? Why indeed – the answer is because of pure liberal politics. As the only two holdouts for constitutionalism over liberal politics on the *Griswold* court, Justices Potter Stewart and Hugo Black[73], asked at 85 S. Ct. 1706:

> "What provision of the Constitution, then, does make this state law invalid? The Court says it is the right of privacy 'created by several fundamental constitutional guarantees '[74]. With all deference, I can find no such general right of privacy in the Bill of Rights, in any other part of the constitution, or in any case ever before decided by this Court. "At the oral argument in this case we were told that the Connecticut law does not 'conform to current community standards.'[75]'But it is not the function of this court to decide cases on the basis of community standards. We are here to decide cases 'agreeable to the Constitution and laws of the United States.' It is the essence of judicial duty to subordinate our own personal views, our own ideas of what legislation is wise and what is not. If, as I should surely hope, the law before us does not reflect the

---

[73] Hugo Black was himself a liberal, but was also a man of integrity who knew his job as a judge and had the courage to do it. Surely a *rara avis* among those on the supreme court bench.

[74] Ah, yes, remember the wet spaghetti approach?

[75] Planned Parenthood's representations were not exactly true, of course, or the Connecticut legislature would have repealed the statute.

standards of the people of Connecticut, the people of Connecticut can freely exercise their true Ninth and Tenth Amendment rights to persuade their elected representatives to repeal it. **That is the constitutional way to take this law off the books.**[76]"[emphasis added]

All the other judges on the Warren court knew that Justices Stewart and Black were right — and almost all judges know it to this day – but liberal political pressure was so intense and the rest of them so weak that they simply caved in to it lest they be deemed 'unenlightened'. This arbitrary invention of new 'constitutional rights' as seen here, and will be seen later in this book regarding subsequent cases, is that constitutional amendments are required to add new rights to (and delete others from) the constitution. The method of doing this is clearly spelled out in Article V of the constitution: a proposed constitutional amendment is voted on by both houses of congress, and, if the proposed amendment passes, it becomes a constitutional amendment. The supreme court knows this, but refuses to require it when it wants to create new rights so as to strike down state laws it doesn't like. For instance, a constitutional amendment was required to create the right of marital privacy, but the court simply invented one so the Connecticut statute could be struck down. Similarly, the right of privacy needed a constitutional amendment, but it was simply more expedient for the court to lie about what it had done in *Griswold* so the right of privacy could be created. The theme goes on and is finally responsible for the supreme court inventing the concept of "liberty interest" to add to the word liberty (which actually is in the constitution), and then to claim that no person could be denied his or her 'liberty interest' with or without due process of law. Such a proposed constitutional amendment would probably not be enacted by congress, so the court simply amends the constitution as it goes along when it so desires.

---

[76] As Planned Parenthood well knows as it had actually tried that and lost thirteen times.

For the bulk of its brief, which I read at the library of congress, Planned Parenthood was content to rely on the same social, political and religious[77] arguments and pleas for enlightenment that it had lost before the Supreme Court of Errors of Connecticut. It lost there and assuredly would have lost in the supreme court if the supreme court hadn't abandoned its position of neutrality and duty to uphold the constitution. At that time Planned Parenthood cited the Lambeth Conference and other "advances in religious thought" as it believed that they supported its case – actually they did support its <u>political argument</u> that could only be properly acted on by a proper legislative body. Their brief was woefully short on the law because there wasn't any law to support their claim that the Connecticut law was unconstitutional. They essentially wound up saying that it was time for a change and hoped that there were enough liberal politicians on the supreme court to agree with them. As the preceding quotation from the dissenting opinion in *Griswold* shows, they were certainly right about that. Add spineless to the list because, liberal or not, and despite dislike of the law and dismay at the Connecticut legislature's refusal to repeal the law when requested to do so thirteen times, the justices' duty was clear – to remain neutral and to follow their oaths of office to uphold the constitution of the United States, even at the risk of being deemed unenlightened by their fellow liberals.

In addition to the fact that it was a total fiction and contrary to the history of the bill of rights, Goldberg's bizarro bill of rights suffered from two other major problems (a) of the millions of retained rights about in the land, how does one determine which ones attain constitutional status? and (b) if the bill of rights was going to be expanded, and since there were many, many retained rights which were important enough to be mentioned in the 158 proposed amendments rejected by the first congress, *Declaration of Independence, Letters From a Pennsylvania*

---

[77] Yes, religious. Although Planned Parenthood vehemently claims that religion has no place in the argument against killing the unborn and no place at all in arguments before the supreme court, it used the Lambeth conference and other "advances in religious thought" in its arguments to the Supreme Court of Errors of Connecticut and to the supreme court when it was advantageous for it to do so..

Farmer, Rights of The British Colonists Asserted And Proved, and *The Federalist Papers,* constitutions of the original thirteen states and so forth that didn't make the constitutional cut, how can this invented "right of marital privacy for family planning" that no document had heretofore even mentioned be catapulted into constitutional status without having to 'wait its turn' along with the other rights that were on the bubble but just missed making the cut? The answer, of course, is pure liberal politics.

ACT II — EISENSTADT VS. BAIRD TRUTH AS A CASUALTY OF THE LEFTWARD SPIRAL

After Arthur Goldberg left the court hoping to influence American policy even more and impose his liberal politics on American society, a new case made its way to the supreme court which was to be the next step in the travesty he started. Although he and Douglas had invented the "right of marital privacy" out of whole cloth and politics, it still left much to be desired from certain liberal groups' points of view: "marital privacy", oddly enough, did not apply to unmarried people because the institution of non-marriage was not also the cornerstone of Western civilization. That seems so self evident that only a politician or a liberal supreme court justice could claim otherwise. This challenge to its goals was met and surmounted by the supreme court in *Eisenstadt v. Baird* [78]. William Baird violated a Massachusetts law against giving a drug or device for the prevention of conception to an unmarried woman. On appeal to the supreme court Baird argued that the Massachusetts law was unconstitutional because he wouldn't have been convicted had he given the vaginal foam to a married woman, and that the right of "marital privacy" should apply also to unmarried women.

Determined though it might be to further impose its political beliefs on America by vetoing yet another valid state statute it didn't like, the court was faced with a few formidable hurdles, some of its

---

[78] *Eisenstadt v. Baird,* 400 U.S. 436. 92 S. Ct. 1029,21 L. Ed. 2d 249 (1972).

own making. There were, or so it would seem, only three possible options here:

1. The first, best and only honest option available was to simply admit that the constitution did not provide for a right of marital privacy after all and to take this opportunity to overrule *Griswold v. Connecticut*. The court could simply have admitted it had been wrong and nobody would ever have to know what it really had been up to. This was the only legally and constitutionally permissible thing to do, but this option was rejected out of hand. Although Goldberg was gone, Douglas was still there and he wasn't about to let any mere constitution interfere with <u>his</u> legacy.

2. Besides being considerably less honest, the second option posed some very high hurdles of its own. Remember the perfidious prosecutor? It had been necessary to prosecute a married woman to so as to allow the court to invent a right of marital privacy since not even Goldberg or Douglas could claim that the institution of non-marriage was the cornerstone of western civilization nor pretend that it also was so fundamental and all pervasive that nobody - not even the *Griswold* court itself bothered to mention it. How, then, did the *Eisenstadt* court plan to do what would have been impossible before marriage became the anointed cornerstone of western civilization?

3. Since the new Amendment 4A to the constitution as pronounced by the *Griswold* court now made it unconstitutional for Massachusetts to pass a statute that made it a crime to distribute vaginal foam to a married woman, and **required** that such a statute be struck down, how could the *Eisenstadt* court reach the conclusion it had set out to reach? The Massachusetts legislature had done <u>exactly</u> what the new improved post-*Griswold* constitution required must be done

by any state legislature that wished to legislate in the area of artificial contraception at all.

Alas, as skilled in the art of judicial doubletalk and non logical thinking as it had become, option three turned out to be an even more insurmountable hurdle for the supreme court than option two had been. As cynical of this bunch as I had understandably become, I never thought that they would simply flat out lie. However, that lie, preceded by some three and a half pages of diversionary material, does appear at 92 S. Ct. 1038:

> "If the right of privacy means anything, it is the right of the *individual*, married or single, to be free from unwarranted governmental intrusion into matters so fundamentally affecting a person as the decision whether to bear or beget a child" [emphasis by the court].

At first blush this seems logical enough: if indeed the new improved post- *Griswold* constitution had provided for the right of individual privacy then, in order to fully implement it, such a right should be available to all individuals regardless of race, color, creed, height or marital status. In fact, if either the original constitution or the new one as improved by the sages on the *Griswold* court provided for the right of non marital or individual privacy [as starkly opposed to "marital privacy"], then distribution of contraceptive devices should be allowed to all. However, another big lie preceded this by just a few lines – the court cited Justice Brandeis' dissent in *Olmstead v. United States* to the effect that there really is such a thing as a constitutional right 'to be let alone'[79] despite the fact that the court knew full well that there was no such right and that Professor Griswold himself acknowledged as

---

[79] As noted previously, all this meant was that Brandeis thought that the Fourth Amendment's requirements for a warrant should be followed, NOT that telephone conversations can never be overheard – anymore than houses can never be searched or that papers can never be seized.

much. The court then simply lied, per Justice William Brennan for the majority, and pretended that *Griswold v. Connecticut* had in fact established a right of individual privacy when in fact the entire fanciful opinion in *Griswold* was based on the facetious claim of Goldberg and Douglas that since the institution of marriage was unique as being the cornerstone of western civilization, the right of marital privacy therefore was so well known and all pervasive that no document in either the history of England or of the United States had bothered to mention it. It was the so-called right of **marital privacy** for the purpose of family planning was that was invented by *Griswold v. Connecticut* and most definitely **NOT** a right of individual or non-marital privacy.

Brennan had actually joined with Goldberg in his concurring opinion in *Griswold* which invented the right of **marital** privacy. As Goldberg had departed to spread his political views on greener pastures, the right of marital privacy was left in the hands of its co-inventors, Brennan and Douglas who were also still on the court. Examining Brennan's intentional misrepresentation of *Griswold's* holding, we find that he doesn't deserve even the weak defense of not knowing any better. Despite having been an active participant in the birthing of the new "right of marital privacy" he nonetheless went on to claim that *Griswold* established the right of individual privacy by making the following gross misrepresentation at 92 S. Ct. 1038:

> "If under *Griswold* the distribution of contraceptives to married persons cannot be prohibited, a ban on distribution to unmarried persons would be equally impermissible. It is true that in *Griswold* the [supposedly individual] **right of privacy** in question **inhered in** the marital relationship." [as if this was just one of those inconsequential coincidences that just sometimes happen as opposed to the very reason the right of marital privacy was invented in the first place.] [emphasis mine]

A much more accurate statement would have been:

"Since under *Griswold* the distribution of contraceptives to married persons cannot be prohibited because of the constitutional right of **marital** privacy, the **only** permissible ban on such distribution would be to persons not protected by the right of marital privacy, to wit, **unmarried people**, and since this Massachusetts statute does only apply to unmarried people as required by our decision in *Griswold v. Connecticut*, this Massachusetts statute is valid."

Brennan may have been a liar[80] but he was no fool. He knew that the only way to reach the conclusion he set out to reach was to start with that very conclusion as his major premise and then appear to reason his way to it. His tautology then is this: "the individual right of privacy is that right of privacy enjoyed by individuals, whether married or not".

Brennan, whose false claim is now that it was the individual's right of privacy that was really at issue in *Griswold* all along, joined in Goldberg's opinion and statements when Goldberg said at 85 S. Ct. 1682," I agree with the Court that Connecticut's birth-control law unconstitutionally intrudes upon the **right of marital privacy**" [emphasis added]. Goldberg and Brennan state further at 85 S. Ct. 1683, " . . . the concept of liberty is not so restricted and that . . .[the concept of liberty] embraces the **right of marital privacy**. . .." [emphasis added]. Brennan also agrees with this whopper that we encountered earlier at 85 S. Ct 1688:

"The entire fabric of the Constitution and the purposes that clearly underlie its specific guarantees demonstrate that the **right of marital privacy** and to marry [are] of

---

[80] William Brennan was, up to this point, an honest, forthright and erudite gentlemen, and was no doubt merely the court's designated liar (DL) here, but the fact that he was a first offender and had cohorts in this misrepresentation scheme does not constitute a defense. While the court was willing to sacrifice the truth and his reputation, he should not have been.

similar order and magnitude as the fundamental rights specifically protected.

★ ★ ★ ★ ★ ★

Although the Constitution does not speak in so many words of the **right of privacy in marriage**, I cannot believe that it offers **these** fundamental rights no protection.. . . The traditional relation of **the family** . . . [is] as old and as fundamental as our entire civilization. . ..” [emphasis added]

All in all, the breakdown is as follows:

Number of times.phrase‘.marital.privacy’.appears. in. *Griswold* 6.
Number of times phrase ‘marital relationship’ appears in *Griswold* 6
Number of times phrase ‘married persons’ appears in *Griswold* 5
Number of times reference is made to ‘ home’ or ‘family in *Griswold* 11
Number of times similar phrases limited to ‘marriage’,’ married couples’,’ husband and wife’ etc. are used in *Griswold* <u>22</u>
    Total references to marriage in *Griswold v. Connecticut* <u>50</u>

Number of times in *Griswold* itself that Brennan, Goldberg or Douglas (or any supreme court justice for that matter) claimed *Griswold* was decided on basis of non marital or individual privacy rights 0

Number of times in *Eisenstadt* Brennan falsely claims that the *Griswold* case was really about <u>individual</u> privacy rights 4

Taking a look back now at the majority opinion in *Griswold,* If Goldberg had just been able to control his penchant for the dramatically untrue, Brennan’s later lie about how *Griswold* supposedly established a right of individual privacy would have been more difficult to pull off. Odd that Brennan himself had joined with Goldberg in sowing the seeds for his own falsehood soon to follow in *Eisenstadt*.

The supreme court justices hold case conferences, and drafts of opinions are circulated to all, so the justices knew that Brennan was to deliver the majority opinion and what he was going to say. Douglas, whose fulminations were almost as frothy and indignant as Goldberg's, was also a holdover from the *Griswold* court. He was the one who raised the specter of government gendarmes running wild by asking the inflammatory rhetorical question, "Would we allow the police to search the <u>sacred precincts of marital bedrooms</u> for telltale signs of the use of contraceptives? The very idea is repulsive to the notions of privacy <u>surrounding the marriage relationship [emphasis added]</u>." Yet the wily old tree hugger remained silent about the real meaning of the *Griswold* case and let Brennan get away with his deception and manipulation of the Fourteenth Amendment to bootstraps a new "constitutional right" into existence. Even if Douglas' theory that the distribution of vaginal foam was just a teaching aid were not so ridiculous, he still should have alerted us to Brennan's falsehoods.[81]

A brief examination of the three and a half pages of diversionary material laid down as cover for Brennan's misrepresentation absolves the court of any accusation of honesty in reaching the political conclusion it had set out to reach. The law—if only it were applicable—laid down as cover is accurate as far as it goes. It sets forth the basic principles governing application of the Equal Protection Clause of the Fourteenth Amendment passed after the civil war. When the court invents or "discovers" a new constitutional right, the cant always is that the discovered right is not new at all, but it had been there all along but somehow managed to escape our notice. This relation back concept would be even <u>greater</u> where the so called right of privacy is concerned because the supreme court specifically claims, on numerous occasions, that the so called right of marital privacy was present before and after Magna Carta in 1215, that it was present before and after all the fundamental documents of the law of England and the

---

[81] According to Douglas' politically motivated stance, shooting a member of the audience after a lecture on the danger of firearms would not be felonious assault because the shooting was just a teaching aid, and conviction of the shooter would violate his First Amendment right of free speech.

American colonies, was present in the Declaration of Independence, the constitution and the Bill of Rights itself! Indeed Goldberg and Douglas claimed the right of marital privacy was part of the anointed cornerstone of Western civilization and was older than civilization itself.

Since this so called constitutional right of marital privacy was supposedly in effect when the Fourteenth Amendment was passed, did the Fourteenth Amendment simply negate it entirely? Of course not. The supreme court didn't seem to think that the equal protection clause prevented it from "discovering" the so called right of marital privacy based on marriage (as opposed to the institution of non marriage) being the cornerstone of western civilization nor required that it die a'borning as the court's bootstraps manipulation of the equal protection clause would have required. So intent was the supreme court on attaining its desired outcome and certain liberal groups' political goals that it was trying to have it both ways: although the *Griswold* decision **requires** that married women and unmarried women be placed into constitutionally different categories for birth control legislation purposes, the *Eisenstadt* decision **forbids** it. This, then, would have been all the more reason for the court to overrule *Griswold* and view the Massachusetts statute on purely equal protection grounds. Not only would those eighteen cited diversionary cases then become applicable, but the court also still could have reached one of its goals of holding the Massachusetts statute unconstitutional – since the Massachusetts classifications would no longer have been required by the overruled *Griswold* case, the statute's classifications could stand or fall on their own merit. The Massachusetts statute then might be be held unconstitutional as a violation of the equal protection clause as there would be no longer be a constitutional requirement for such classification. Since, however, the so called right of marital privacy was still there, and by definition and its own terms, applied only to married persons and also required that unmarried persons be treated differently, how can it possibly be attacked by still later supreme court's intentional misapplications of the equal protection clause? The answer is that it obviously can't be and the three and a half pages of diversionary law were known to be inapplicable at the time they were used to mislead the unwary.

None of those 18 cited cases even dealt with constitutionally mandated classifications, **NONE** (!) of them support the supreme court's position, and most of the cited cases are actually AGAINST it. The first cited case of *Reed v. Reed*.[82] involved an Idaho statute that preferred male executors to female executors in probating estates. Since nothing in United States constitution either permitted or **required** that males be preferred to females in the order of probating estates, the court was free to look at the basis for, and reasonableness of, such preference. The basis for the preference was that it would ease the work burden on the probate courts by eliminating an extra hearing. Laudable as that goal might be, the supreme court then looked at the reasonableness of the classification and decided that women were equally as capable as men of acting as executors of estates, and therefore the classification and the statute were invalid. I doubt if anyone would argue with the supreme court on this as long as the constitution did not require such a preference.

Another cited case which supported upholding the Massachusetts statute that the court so eagerly struck down in *Eisenstadt* was *Shapiro v. Thompson* [83]. The states there involved had all imposed residency requirements upon the receipt of welfare benefits under federal law. The court said that attaching residency requirements to the receipt of welfare benefits would discourage prospective recipients of public funds from moving from one state to another to collect benefits.[84] . Examining the basis for separating prospective recipients into two classes, (1) those who already lived in the state and (2) those who recently moved into the state for the purpose of receiving the benefits, the court found that there was no basis for the classification that would stand up to the requirements of the equal protection clause of the Fourteenth Amendment. The cases stands for the often

---

[82] *Reed V. Reed*, 414U.S, 71, 75-76, 92 S. Ct, 351, 253, 30 L. Ed 2d 223 (1971)

[83] *Shapiro v. Thompson*, 394 U.S.618, 89 S. Ct. 1322, 22 L. Ed 2d 600 (1969).

[84] Actually, that was the reason these residency requirements were passed in the first place.

repeated proposition that congress cannot authorize or require states to separate people into those categories as that would be a violation of the equal protection clause. While that is true, it is also true that only the constitution _itself_ can either allow or require that such otherwise objectionable classifications be made. It wasn't congress that allowed the Massachusetts legislature to draw a distinction between married women and unmarried women – it was the improved post-_Griswold_ constitution that required it. It wasn't congress that required that any state that wished to pass a criminal law against use of contraceptive devices could only pass one that applied to unmarried women – it was a requirement mandated by the post-_Griswold_ constitution. Since three of the members of the _Griswold v. Connecticut_ court were still on the _Eisenstadt_ court that ruled that it was unconstitutional for Massachusetts to follow the post-_Griswold_ mandate the supreme court itself had created, could they honestly have forgotten what they themselves had so recently decided and required?

The reader can easily prove the supreme court wrong by asking him or herself the following two questions:

(1) Would the Massachusetts statute in _Eisenstadt_ have been held unconstitutional even if _Griswold_ had never been decided? It may have been because, while neither married nor unmarried women would have had a constitutional right to marital privacy, the reason the statute would have been unconstitutional could have simply been that since the different classifications were not required by the constitution as newly improved by _Griswold_, they were a violation of the equal protection clause. The idea of marital privacy wouldn't have been a factor at all as it was irrelevant.

(2) Did, for instance, the equal protection clause of the fourteenth amendment passed in 1866 give women the right to vote or was in necessary that the nineteenth amendment be passed in 1920 for that to happen? Of course it was necessary that the constitution be amended by the nineteenth amendment for

this to happen. By the same token, the newly invented right of marital privacy did not automatically become the right of non marital privacy by virtue of the equal protection clause – it was necessary that a constitutional amendment so stating be adopted. Logical considerations like this don't seem to faze the supreme court at all when it sets out to achieve a goal it resolved to reach BEFORE the case is even decided. .

(3) *Griswold* 's only true bearing on the *Eisenstadt* case was that it **required** the very classification that the court claimed was forbidden by the equal protection clause, and consequently it was the *Griswold* case itself that **required** that the Massachusetts statute be **upheld!** Talk about being foist on your own petard!

SUMMARY SO FAR

1) No document in the history of England, colonial America or the United States even mentions the so called "right of marital privacy";

2) *Entick v. Carrington* and *Wilkes v. Wood* concerned only the property right of freedom from unreasonable searches and seizures and the personal right of freedom from unreasonable and arbitrary arrest;

3) None of the thirteen state constitutions mention the so called "right of marital privacy";

4) A motion to include a bill of rights in the constitution was tabled and the motion to add one after it was drafted was defeated unanimously;

5) Article Four of the draft of the constitution (which can be seen in the National Archives) reserving to the states all powers not specifically granted to congress was crossed out and did

not become part of the constitution as the framers wanted no restrictions at all on the new congress;

6) After the constitution almost failed to be ratified, Madison was forced to include a bill of rights after all. Over two hundred amendments were suggested to the first federal congress, but neither the so called "right of marital privacy" nor so called "right of individual privacy" were among them. The framers of the constitution wanted liberties protected through the political process, not the judicial one[85];

7) Advocates for repeal of the Connecticut statute, correctly recognizing that the birth control pill issue is purely a political one, have thirteen bills introduced in Connecticut legislature that would have repealed the laws against artificial means of birth control. All bills lose as the Connecticut legislature makes the unwise political decision not to repeal the birth control laws;

8) The perfidious prosecutor and a certain liberal group arrange to have that group and three married women prosecuted for using birth control pills as that would give the prosecutor his only chance of losing the case, a goal both sides shared;

9) The Connecticut courts rightly refuse Planned Parenthood's request to invent a right of marital privacy for it so that the birth control law would be unconstitutional. The Supreme Court of Errors of Connecticut quite rightly tells Planned Parenthood to have this purely political question decided by the state legislature;

10) The United States Supreme Court, acting as a super legislature in *Griswold v. Connecticut*, custom invents the so called "right of

---

[85] Rene de Visme Williamson, *Political Process or Judicial Process: The Bill of Rights and The Framers of The Constitution*, Journal of Politics 23 (1961), as stated in *Context of the Bill of Rights*, op cit, p. 73

marital privacy" for Planned Parenthood as requested. Although they dislike the outdated Connecticut law as much as the others do, only Justices Hugo Black and Potter Stewart have the courage to remain neutral and dissent from the majority's caving in to political pressure;

11) In *Eisenstadt v. Baird*, Justice William Brennan lies about the decision in *Griswold*, saying that the *Griswold* case was really about <u>individual</u> privacy all along as opposed to <u>marital</u> privacy, and therefore claims that the so called "right of marital privacy" was merely properly extended to unmarried persons to become the new so called "right of individual privacy";

12) Contrary to the *Eisenstadt* court's claim, the post-*Griswold* constitution not only prohibited a ban on the distribution of contraceptive devices to married women, it also **required** that for legislation to be upheld, it **must** apply to unmarried women only. Consequently, in order to create a right of individual or non-marital privacy, a constitutional amendment must be passed.

The stage was now set for the long planned assault on the nation's abortion laws[86]

ACT II — ROE VS. WADE IGNORANCE AND POLITICS VS. REALITY

Texas Penal Code section 19.02 CAPITAL MURDER "(a) A person commits an offense if the person commits a murder as defined in sec. 19.02(b)(1) and (3) the person commits the murder for remuneration

---

[86] These plans hark back to the very founding of Planned Parenthood by Margaret Sanger who planned to have abortions performed on poor people, especially poor black people, serve the eugenic movement's goal of ridding the population of what she and Planned Parenthood viewed as an unwanted segment of society so as to 'purify the stock'.

or employs another to commit the murder for remuneration or the promise of remuneration

Texas Penal Code section 19.03: TYPES OF CRIMINAL HOMICIDE. (a) a person commits criminal homicide if he intentionally . . . causes the death of an individual" (b) " Criminal homicide is murder, capital murder, manslaughter or criminally negligent homicide."

Murder is usually broken down into first degree which requires premeditation, second degree which is less planned and more spontaneous, and manslaughter which is an unjustified killing committed in the heat of passion: the most heinous of these crimes is first degree murder. Because it requires premeditation, classic examples are murder by poisoning and by ambush. A person must plan to kill, plan to obtain the poison, obtain the poison, and then either inject it into the victim or put the poison in the victim's food or drink. This cannot be done spontaneously or in the heat of passion during an argument. By the same token, the criminal cannot accidently plan to intercept the victim while he is on a journey and then shoot him with a loaded rifle he 'just happened' to have brought with him from his home many miles away: the assassination of President Kennedy is a good example of this type of murder.

The only type of premeditation that is greater than murder by poison or lying in wait is first degree murder by abortion. There the killing is thought about and planned for some time, a hit man is hired, an appointment is made for the killing and then the fatal appointment is kept. It doesn't get any more premeditated than this. Oddly, abortion advocates stress the amount of premeditation as a justification for the killing, as if that somehow makes the victim less dead or the act less heinous. As every law student and supreme court justice knows, the only defenses that would make an intentional killing not be a murder are (1) war (2) self defense and (3) the defense of others.[87]

Notwithstanding the fact that hundreds of thousands of these

---

[87] The possible fourth defense, insanity, does not fully fall in this category of confession and avoidance since the 'sanity' of the accused is really a factor to be taken into account in determining whether the defendant had the capacity to form the requisite intent in the first place.

murders were committed annually, prosecutors throughout the country were reluctant to file murder charges against the hit men because the penalties were so severe. Many states sought to decrease the number of these killings and to increase the likelihood of prosecution by drastically reducing the penalties. One such state was Texas which reduced the penalty for murder by abortion from execution to a short term of imprisonment. Articles 1191-1194 and 1196 of the Texas penal code made it a crime, punishable by only imprisonment for a term of two to five years, to administer to a pregnant woman any drug that would cause an abortion or to cause an abortion by violence. A single woman (Roe[88]) brought a class action challenging the statute reducing the penalty for murder by abortion. Despite the facts that Texas' state constitution empowers its legislature to pass a penal code, and that its murder statute had been in effect for over one hundred years, the supreme court held that Texas could not reduce the penalty for murder by abortion by passing a law that specifically prohibits abortions. The basis for this is almost as convoluted as Goldberg's near hallucinogenic opinion in *Griswold v. Connecticut.*

Many states, Texas, Michigan and Minnesota among them, provide that a negligent automobile driver who causes the wrongful death of a pregnant woman and her preborn child in an automobile crash faces two wrongful death lawsuits – one brought on behalf of the mother and one brought on behalf of the baby. The baby's right to remain alive is not in any way derivative of the mother's right to remain alive because the negligent driver is still liable for the baby's wrongful death even if the mother survives. This is the case also in criminal law—when the criminal murders both the expectant mother and her preborn baby, he will be convicted of both murders. The baby's right to remain alive is in no way derivative of the mother's right to remain alive because the shooter will still be convicted of one murder even if the mother survives. While It has been widely known since well before the civil war that life begins at conception, it was not known conclusively that life begins at fertilization until 1875 when Oscar

---

[88] Actually, Norma Corvey, who now favors upholding state laws against abortion.

Hertwig and Herman Fol, each working independently, showed that the essential act of fertilization is not union of the two cells, ovum and sperm as once thought, but the actual fusion of the two nuclei into one, with the offspring beginning its life as a combination of the nuclei of its two parents.[89] The long time president of Planned Parenthood— and consequently Planned Parenthood itself — acknowledged this indisputable fact in 1933, many <u>years</u> before Planned Parenthood and the supreme court tried to profess ignorance of it in *Roe v. Wade*[90]. The various states statutes which reduced the penalties for first degree murder by abortion were soundly backed by the cutting edge biology of 1875, and needless to say, all the medical evidence from 1875 to 1973 which conclusively showed that the various states' whose statutes were predicated on the premise that life begins at fertilization were absolutely correct.

Federal law is different in the sense that there really was no' federal law' on the subject at all before 1973 for two reasons (1) congress had not been granted power to legislate in the area of abortion at all and had not yet tried to get away with doing so[91]and (2) the well known case of *Erie v. Tompkins* [92] requires that Federal District Courts follow the substantive law of the state where they are sitting while federal procedural law (court rules, rules of evidence, etc.) is followed in all federal district courts. Why, then, should federal law be different in this area, especially when the constitution in **two separate places** provides for the right to life, the right to life appears in our Declaration of Independence, in James Otis' "The Rights of the British Colonists

---

[89] Alan Frank Guttmacher, *Life In The Making* (Garden City, New Jersey and New York, Garden City Publishing Co., Inc. 1933), p.43

[90] The editors of both leading medical dictionaries have recently backed away from this truth, claiming that life really doesn't begin at fertilization after all, but is on hold until implantation up to three days later when pregnancy begins. This was done so as to facilitate the use of the morning after kill pill, and to ease the consciences of those doing the killing.

[91] Congress, however, has tried to exceed its granted powers since that time, the latest attempt before Obamacare being the Usurpation of Criminal Law Act of 2009 (sometimes euphemistically called Freedom of Choice Act or FOCA).

[92] *Erie v. Tompkins*, 304 U.S, 64, 58 S Ct 817, 82 L Ed 1188.

Asserted and Proved" and the English Declaration of Rights of 1689, whereas the so called right of marital privacy appears in none of them? There is no good answer to this question other than "it certainly shouldn't be and wouldn't be were it not for politics and judicial cowardice". The culprit as to how things came to pass is once again the supreme court.

The only question that needed to be decided by the supreme court in *Roe v. Wade*[93] was this: at what stage of life does the constitutional right to life attach – when life begins or at some future arbitrary time? Not even the left could justify a decision that came right out and said that the constitutional right to life does not attach when life begins, but rather attaches at some future arbitrary time, for to do that would be to admit that the bestowing of the mantle of 'personhood actually **IS** the modern day equivalent of quickening. Unfortunately the supreme court had become quite slippery and adept at ducking the main issues in these cases and recasting them is such a way that made its desired answer marginally less absurd.

As the court admits at several places in the majority opinion, if the right to remain alive attaches when life begins, then Texas statute outlawing abortions would have to be upheld. This suggested the other side of the coin – if life didn't begin until three weeks after conception, then abortions before that time could be permitted. If life didn't begin until 'quickening (thought by people in the middle ages to be at around the twenty fifth week of the pregnancy term), then only post-quickening abortions could be prohibited. By this elastic standard, if the preborn baby was a mass of lifeless cells, or as Hillary Clinton and the supreme court put it, only a 'potential life', and did not magically spring into life until the moment of birth, then all state statutes making the intentional killing of a preborn baby before that magical moment a crime would be unconstitutional. The outcome sought by supreme court could have been much more easily reached before 1875 because, until then, no one could really pinpoint the exact moment that life began. Unfortunately for Planned Parenthood and

---

[93] *Roe v. Wade* 410 U.S. 959, 93 S. Ct. 1409, 35 L. Ed. 147 (1973)

the supreme court, it had been conclusively determined in 1875 that life indeed does begin at fertilization. Despite that uncontestable fact, the supreme court thought it would be helpful to treat the reader to a review of how various people felt about abortion <u>before</u> they knew when life began. Actually the attitude of various people and societies throughout history is IMMATERIAL for two reasons: first and foremost, it could only have a marginal bearing if indeed we were still ignorant of when life began. Unlike some, the vast [94]majority of educated people in the world knew—and had known for almost a hundred years—that life begins at fertilization. Indeed, the word foetus itself means "little person" in Latin. All physicians, including those employed by Justice Harry Blackmun's former client, the Mayo Clinic, knew that life begins at fertilization because all United States medical schools taught this uncontestable fact.[95]Shortly after it became a state, the Texas legislature reduced the penalties for murder by abortion in 1859 by passing the statute under attack. It's hard to see during just what brief time period the right to kill a preborn baby managed to become "deeply rooted in the traditions and conscience of our people"[96]. As Justice Rehnquist points out in his dissenting opinion, this alleged "right" was totally unknown to the drafters of the Fourteenth Amendment (drafted in 1866), let alone to the framers of the constitution. Of the thirty six states that had statutes similar to the statute Texas had at the time reducing the penalties for this type of intentional killing, the first was enacted by Connecticut in 1821 – just thirty two years after the founding of this country— and the last was enacted by Florida in 1860[97] — all thirty six statutes were enacted **even**

---

[94] There are still a few hard core ideologues at Planned Parenthood who, even in 2011, cling to the pixie dust fiction that life does not begin until the baby crosses the plane of the vaginal goal line.

[95] Justice Blackmun was chief counsel of the Mayo Clinic before becoming a supreme court justice.

[96] The then-current test as to how an alleged right makes the trip from the bizarro bill of rights to the real one.

[97] These were state and territorial laws in effect before the Fourteenth Amendment was enacted in 1868. Of these, twenty one were still in effect when the Texas statute was struck down as being one of thirty seven such state statutes contrary to the so

before it was conclusively established that life begins at fertilization! The second reason that the supreme court's tour down memory lane is pointless is that we are talking about deeply rooted traditions the people of Texas, not of the people of England, ancient Athens, Persia or even of the thirty six states of the United States which – contrary to what the import of the supreme court's argument would appear to suggest – agreed with Texas.

It appears that Blackmun, ignoring anything he may have learned from the Mayo clinic about when life begins as well as ignoring any biology he might have picked up in high school, professes to be one of the few people on the planet who doesn't know when life begins. In its amicus brief in *Roe* and even today, Planned Parenthood professes ignorance of when life begins. Why, were it not for the fortunate spreading of pixie dust at the last minute, all babies would be stillborn! Aside from disregarding another forty five years of post-*Roe* conclusive and dramatic evidence, it and the supreme court in *Roe* overlooked that fact that the long time president and patron saint of Planned Parenthood, Alan Frank Guttmacher, had written a book called 'Life in the Making' in 1933 that not only acknowledges this fact on numerous occasions but also chides the rest of humanity for taking so long to understand this. While expressing dismay that it took the human race so long to figure out when life begins, at least he was confident in 1933 that no one could ever claim otherwise. No wait, Guttmacher did later decide that the intentional killing of a preborn baby was alright, didn't he?

Now, it is possible for a person to change his opinion or political position, but could Guttmacher really change the inconvenient truth he himself had so recently trumpeted? Could the organization of which he was president have claimed ignorance of this well established, incontestable and <u>admitted</u> fact when it was professing ignorance of it in 1973? Of course not. It is well established law that a corporation or organization functions by its members, officers and employees, and

called deeply rooted right to commit murder by abortion (Michigan having reduced the penalty for first degree murder by abortion to a short term of years by ballot initiative in 1972).

that notice and knowledge to its members, officers and employees is notice and knowledge to the organization itself. That leads to the following observation:

> "While books may be written that are lacking in tact
> Only Alan Frank Guttmacher can unknow a fact"

To the surprise of no one, the supreme court didn't let this fundamental principle of law, evidence and common sense regarding knowledge stand between it and the conclusion it set out to reach. We are treated to several pages of a meaningless meander wherein we learn that while not himself a Pythagorean[98], Hippocrates was unduly influenced by them, and so the Hippocratic oath was really a "Pythagorean manifesto" 93 S. Ct. 716 . I doubt that this means that 80 generations of physicians didn't actually take an oath not to procure abortions because when they did they may not have fully realized the impact of Pythagorean philosophy on the 'Father of Medicine', but perhaps the court meant that had there been fewer Pythagoreans to worry about, maybe Hippocrates would have written the oath differently, and then maybe 80 generations of physicians would have made a different promise. How could seven out of nine supreme court justices, all whom had graduated from high school, even entertain the outrageous idea that twentieth century United States Constitutional Law should be determined by the number of non-Pythagorean Greek physicians who disagreed with Hippocrates 2,500 years ago?

Even without the benefits of modern medicine and modern knowledge, the Pythagoreans guessed right because life indeed does begin at conception. They knew that the embryo was animate [infused with life or 'animus'] from the moment of conception, and therefore abortion was the destruction of a living person. Many of Hippocrates' Athenian contemporaries around 400 B.C. didn't back the Pythagoreans on this and apparently ignored Hippocrates. After the Romans stopped persecuting the Christians, Christian ideas resurrected the Hippocratic

---

[98] Oh, those pesky Pythagoreans

oath and the philosophy of the Pythagoreans because life, indeed, does begin at conception. The court's reference to the Romans is particularly odd since, as Taswell-Langmead points out in" The Constitutional History of England":

> "It is certain that the principles of our [British unwritten] constitution are in no wise derived from either Celt or Roman. The civilization of the Romans, for the most part, departed with them"[99]

Presumably, the last of the non-Pythagorean Greeks departed with them also. Some time thereafter the 'quickening' problem set in. As it turns out there is no such thing as a distinction between a preborn baby which is quick and one which is less quick, but the legal difference lingered on for awhile despite this knowledge. Although the Pythagoreans, ancient Persians, Texans and most of the other states in the United States guessed right, the fact that the Aztecs, some ancient Greeks and others guessed wrong has been a moot point ever since 1875 when the Pythagoreans were conclusively proved right by Hertwig, Fol, and by all the medical evidence since then. The court, however, seems to subscribe to this liberal bootstraps logic argument:

> Since it was not known until 1875 that life begins at fertilization, a state statute before that time that prohibited abortions would probably have been held unconstitutional as we would have thought it would have interfered with a woman's right of marital privacy[100]. The fact that we now know that life indeed does begin at fertilization does nothing to change that

---

[99] Theodore Plunckett, MA, LLB, MA Litt, *Taswell-Langmead's English Constitutional History* (11th ed.). Boston, Houghton Mifflin Co. 1960, p. 2.
[100] Assuming, of course, that the 'right of marital privacy' had been invented sometime before 1875.

since we didn't know that fact until it was discovered,[101] and we like our first answer better anyway. A much better argument – and the only logically and legally possible one would be:

"If life began some time after fertilization, then only Those state statutes which prohibited abortions before life began would be unconstitutional. Now that we know when life begins, all state statutes that make committing the crime of abortion after fertilization are valid and will be upheld."

Michigan and almost all the other states correctly recognize that preborn babies are in fact alive – that's why wrongful death claims and murder prosecutions can proceed against all perpetrators of these murders except the ones hired by the victims' mothers. The supreme court has simply declared that the mother's right to privacy trumps the baby's right to life. To weasel out of this naked truth, the court actually called the baby's life a "potential life" at 93 S. Ct. 732. This outright falsehood was adopted by the court in *Planned Parenthood v. Casey* at 112 S. Ct 2799 and still later by Hillary Clinton in her 2008 presidential campaign. Why a preborn baby has more life potential at eight months after conception that it does at one month after conception is not fully explained, unless the court is just quoting body count statistics— in that case, a baby who has successfully run the gauntlet of death for eight months probably does have a better chance of survival than does one who is just starting it.

One of the several things that the court ignored here was the hypothetical case known to every first year criminal law student, that of the pushed man. If a person were to push another off the top of the Empire State building and the second person fell to his death, the pusher would be guilty of murder. If, however, a gunman on the ninety second floor were to shoot and kill that falling person, the

---

[101] This type of thinking appeared in a Nancy Pelosi press conference wherein she tried to justify her pro abortion position.

shooter [not the pusher] would be guilty of murder, even though the odds of surviving the fall were virtually nil. We do have rather an interesting twist on that classic hypothetical: here the abortionist plays the role of both the pusher _and_ the shooter. In any event, it doesn't matter a whole lot whether the hit man is playing the pusher or the shooter role as he intentionally caused the death in any event. The key here is that the supreme court is saying that the victim's mother was merely exercising her so called right of privacy when she hired the hit man, so he is cloaked with her immunity.

We discussed earlier that the common law approach, whatever its considerable merits may be regarding the development of the common law and constitutional law of a nation that does not have a constitution, is not really applicable to the constitutional law of a country that does have a written constitution. In fact, that's why our constitution was and is praised by almost everyone except Woodrow Wilson, Roscoe Pound, Barney Frank, most liberals[102] and all progressives. However, once the mistake was made to use the common law approach, the court, rather than cherry picking which part should be used, should have utilized the true genius of the common law approach – weighing and balancing. The process of weighing and balancing has always been part of the common law; it goes on even today although at such a slow pace that we usually don't know that it's happening. The one exception to this is an injunction hearing. There the main questions when the rights of one person are in conflict with the rights of another are: (a) whether a reasonable compromise can be worked out that would accommodate both sets of rights which seem to be in conflict and (b) if not, which rights should prevail? The correct answer must also take into account (c) which injury is irreparable? Since there is no way to reassemble and resurrect an aborted baby and there is no injury more

---

[102] This brings up the curious status of the liberal ACLU. The ACLU passionately defends those parts of the constitution with which it agrees politically, but just as passionately defends the supreme court's blatant disregard for the constitution in the area of the so called right of privacy and right to killing by abortion. Justice Ruth Bader Ginsburg is the former chief counsel for the ACLU.

irreparable than death, the baby's right to remain alive must clearly prevail for this reason also.

Applying the test to the only real issue in *Roe v. Wade*, we find that there is a perfectly good compromise that can be worked out that would accommodate both sets of rights, that is, adoption (and as I write this, there are 48 sets of prospective adoptive parents for every baby available for adoption). Only the slightest detriment to the mother's' right of privacy'[103] would be involved in that she would remain pregnant for only a few months longer. Once placed for adoption, the baby's constitutional right to remain alive for the next eighty three years can also be accommodated. Strangely, an adoption plan is usually rejected out of hand by the mother who would prefer to live with the guilt that her selfishness killed her child rather than with the knowledge that her compassion and heroism saved its life, and it is not counseled for by the proprietor of the killing field. The supreme court could easily decide that's what should be done, but has opted for a brinkmanship type confrontational approach.[104] If this approach should fail, the next part of the common law that actually <u>is</u> its true genius – the weighing and balancing test—would kick in. If you were to believe the ubiquitous bumper stickers telling legislators to 'Get Your Laws Off My Body', then the only thing the so called right to privacy impacts is about five additional months of pregnancy. Awarding the mother two points per month for this, her side of the balance scale would now have ten (10) points. Even assuming the baby's right to remain alive is worth no more than two points per month, the baby still has two thousand and two (2,002) points on its side of the balance scale. But shouldn't life itself be awarded more points than the freedom from the discomfort of

---

[103] Assuming, for the sake of this argument only, that there really is such a thing as a constitutional right of privacy.

[104] Defenders of the court might argue that that's not the way things are usually done and it would therefore not be the court's usual procedure. It is, however, greatly preferable to the abandonment of neutrality, disregarding of the justices' oaths of office, the outcome driven decisions, routine caving in to political pressure and outright lying that has been so much a part of the supreme court majority's decisions in this area. Also the supreme court <u>does</u> have the power to change the court rules, and so accomplishing this would present no problem at all.

pregnancy? If one thousand (1,000) points are awarded for each of the nine hundred ninety six months of the baby's life, the score becomes one million one thousand (1,001,000) to ten (10) in favor of the baby.

At this point, the court and others might abandon the pretense that it is only five months of pregnancy which are involved and acknowledge that it is really the impact on lifestyle and the expense of raising a child that have always been the key ingredients here – 'they're expensive to raise, so they've got one foot in the grave'! At any rate, if the goal is to avoid those expenses and avoid parental responsibilities, the first question to arise is: since all states have laws designed to prevent the avoidance of parental responsibilities, why should any points at all be awarded for this noble goal? The correct answer is that none should be, but at least Planned Parenthood and the supreme court will have had to acknowledge that money is what this has always been all about[105]. However, even if we award an additional two points per month for avoidance of parental responsibilities, the baby still wins by the slam dunk of one million one thousand (1,001,000) to four hundred forty two (442).

Using the time honored weighing and balancing test would not, however, get the supreme court where it wanted to go, and so we are treated to several pages of verbiage to the effect that state legislatures have a sufficient interest to pass laws prohibiting the intentional killing of preborn babies during the last three months of the pregnancy term, have enough of an interest to 'regulate' the killings during the middle three months, but lack a sufficient interest in doing either during the first three months of the pregnancy term. The second question in all this is whether the date on which a life is taken really has any significance at all? The answer, of course, is that it has no significance whatsoever, but the even more important question is why has the "state's interest" been substituted for the baby's right to life? The answer to this question is that otherwise it would be a slam dunk for

---

[105] To say nothing of the huge sums involved in abortion fees and federal subsidies to the abortion industry.

the baby, so the only way to veto the statute is to claim the state lacked "sufficient interest" and authority to pass it in the first place.

Imagine this dim witted approach in another context where court sanctimoniously intones that:

> "The state has sufficient interest in preventing armed robberies at night to prohibit them altogether, has enough interest in preventing afternoon armed robberies to regulate them, but insufficient interest in preventing morning armed robberies to pass a law against them at all.

The Blackmun court took us for fools in *Roe v. Wade* and the current court has done nothing to change that.

ACT IV — PLANNED PARENTHOOD VS. CASEY POLITICS TRIUMPHS YET AGAIN

Next in this line of political decisions was *Planned Parenthood v. Casey*[106]. At issue were five provisions of Pennsylvania's statute regulating abortions, some of which the court found to "unduly burden" a woman's so called right to have an abortion and which were therefore struck down, and some whose burden was not so undue and which were allowed to stand. Before proceeding with the work at hand, the court felt it necessary do some house cleaning and revisionism. So anxious were the previous courts in *Griswold, Eisenstadt* and *Roe v. Wade* itself to adopt certain liberal groups' political programs that the most charitable thing that could be said about the supreme court's opinions in this area is that, besides being unquestionably wrong, they were less than models of clarity. For instance, and assuming that there actually was a constitutional basis for the decision in *Griswold*, what was it?

Douglas, as we have seen, took the wet spaghetti approach – just

---

[106] *Planned Parenthood v. Casey* 505 U.S. 833. 112 S. Ct. 2791, 120 L. Ed, 2d. 2791 (1992).

throw a lot of things out there and hope that some of them stick to the wall or at least give the illusion of sticking. Now there's certainly nothing wrong with articulating several legal bases for a decision – as long as there **are** several bases. When there is only one basis, a good technique is to rely on that one and then buttress your position by saying that your view finds support in several different areas [prior court opinions, etc.] The catch here is that you have to have **at least one** legal leg to stand on. If only one argument is used and that one argument qualifies as a constitutional basis for a decision, then that is a perfectly valid approach as well. When none of the strands of wet spaghetti make the grade, however, the only possible thing to do is to decide the case the other way. Since none of Douglas' arguments passed the test, the only constitutional thing to do was to uphold the Connecticut statute, even though this would not bring about the hoped-for result. You can liken each argument to that test your strength game they have at county fairs – you swing the mallet, striking it against the pad, and the marker goes up a certain distance. If the marker goes up far enough, you are declared a winner and awarded a prize.

Using a scale of one to ten where a score of at least nine is necessary to be achieved In order to qualify as a constitutional right, we find that Douglas' and Goldberg's false history of the bill of rights merits a two; Douglas's helper rights argument is lucky to get a two since it deliberately confuses specific and general rights as well as substantive and procedural rights, and ignores the reason for true helper rights altogether; Douglas' Fourth and Fifth Amendment arguments get a three because the right of marital privacy simply isn't there; Douglas's penumbra argument scores highest at a four; Goldberg's and Douglas' grade school argument that a right of marital privacy is proven because it was never mentioned at all until the supreme court coined that phrase gets a two; Goldberg's Ninth Amendment argument gets a zero since all three prior ninth amendment cases were against him and he knew it – this was overrulement by stealth and guile; Goldberg's bizarro bill of rights argument gets a zero also as it is directly contrary to the history of the bill of rights and wouldn't have made sense even if he hadn't deliberately falsified the history; his "all the privacies of life" argument fails as that dicta never became part of our constitution nor was it a basis for his decision; and his "right to be let alone" argument fails also and it wasn't even supported by Professor Griswold in his graduation speech (these last two, however, were slipped in so that Brennan could later more easily lie about the basis for the *Griswold* decision.)[107]

All these attempts do show, however, just how eager the court was to reach the political result it sought. Aside from the fact that none of the wet spaghetti arguments made the top of the wall, they really don't sound that appealing when compared to the Fourteenth Amendment. The only problem is that the *Griswold* case **wasn't** decided by dusting off the obsolete 'substantive due process' argument and bringing it out of retirement. Once incorporation had been achieved in 1948 by making the rights actually in the bill of rights applicable to the states as well, the due process argument was no longer operative – and this was made very clear by the court — and it had never before been used to make a newly invented 'right' applicable to the states.

To use the Fourteenth Amendment would present yet another obstacle to the supposedly neutral and objective supreme court accomplishing its goal: the due process clause unquestionably supports the right to life., for it is the right to life itself that a person can't be deprived of without due process of law! The court skated around this problem by simply ignoring it altogether.

This manufactured disguise of what the actual basis for *Griswold* and *Roe v. Wade* was in full muddle when the *Casey* court 'clarified' all that by rewriting history and saying at 112 S. Ct. 2804 that:

---

[107] Goldberg's and Brennan's defenders could claim that Brennan had not yet formed the intent to lie in as much as that neither knew when a case like *Eisenstadt* would come before the court, and so facilitation of a later falsehood was not, therefore, the purpose of throwing in these two alleged "rights" of totally different etiologies. No one can deny, however, that the inclusion of these two arguments which had nothing to do with 'marital privacy' certainly did facilitate Brennan's later misrepresentation.

> "Constitutional protection of the woman's decision to terminate her pregnancy[108] derives from the Due Process Clause of the Fourteenth Amendment. It declares that no State shall 'deprive any person of **LIFE** [109], liberty, or property, without due process of law.'" [emphasis added]

This is where the housekeeping and revisionism come in. Douglas' fiat and the near hallucinogenic verbiage of Goldberg's opinion regarding "marital privacy" had already been spun into the even more novel concept of "non-marital privacy" on the magic loom of *Eisenstadt v. Baird,* while Goldberg's bizarro bill of rights and third grade argument about how the fact that something isn't there proves that it is because it must have been so obvious that nobody bothered to write it down had understandably become an embarrassment, so why not just pretend that *Griswold* had always been a Fourteenth Amendment case all along? If this were done, the court needn't be troubled with all the inconsistencies, contradictions, feeble attempts at legal reasoning, naked politics and downright falsehoods that it had grown so used to dealing in. That was such a good idea that the court lost no time in embracing it. Actually this would have been a great time to seize the opportunity of simply overruling *Griswold v. Connecticut* and *Roe v. Wade* even at the risk of being deemed unenlightened. Chief Justice Rehnquist nailed it when he tried to seize this opportunity to return to the constitution at the expense of politics, but he was heavily outvoted. Aside from the judicial doubletalk about the basis for the *Griswold v. Connecticut* decision, would it really have mattered? Perhaps this was just a harmless little game of three card monty designed to make the court look a bit less foolish. Well, yes, it would have made all the difference in the world and would have prevented the supreme court from reaching the outcome it set out to reach. Unfortunately

---

[108] Referred to by one hit man as being ". . . when the woman elects to deliver early". This is the usual definition of a C-section.

[109] Ironic, isn't it, that the clause that the supreme court pretends that it relied on is the very clause that **guarantees** the right to life?

these cases were decided the way cheaters solve a maze. The correct way – and the way a court is supposed to operate – is to examine the outside of the maze to see if there is a way in. If there is, you then follow that lead wherever it takes you: if you arrive at the center, then so be it – you have solved the maze and gotten an answer. If, however, the chosen path leads to a dead end, you either have to start over or give up and decide the case the other way. But the supreme court — neutral and objective as it no doubt was — simply started at the center and worked its way backward to find out what the best way was to say how it got there.

The technique of doing one thing while saying that it was doing something else had served the court well in the past, and so it was trotted out again. In *Griswold,* before acting as a super-legislature by vetoing a statute it didn't like, the court said at 85 S. Ct. 1680 that, "We do not sit as a super-legislature to determine the wisdom, need, and propriety of laws . ...", and then proceeded to do exactly that. Thinking that such disclaimers would again be helpful, the supreme court tried it again in *Casey.* Before again caving in to political pressure, the *Casey* court said at 112 U.S. 2798 that it should not, and does not, cave in to political pressure. Just the opposite, however, is true: the decisions in *Griswold, Eisenstadt, Roe* and now *Casey* were the very embodiment of caving in to political pressure . The court noted that deciding *Roe v. Wade* had been divisive and that overruling it would be also as it would disappoint certain groups. Such anticipated reactions by others certainly does seem like politics, although the group that was 'disappointed' in 1973 when *Roe* was decided and the constitution ignored was much larger then than was the group that would have been disappointed in 1992 were the *Casey* court to follow the constitution. The 1992 group which favored murder by abortion, though smaller than the group that opposed these killings and would uphold the constitution, was the one in whose eyes the justices dearly wished to be deemed 'enlightened', and so politics once again ruled the day and the decision.

Political cowardice, although the real driver, wasn't the only reason the *Casey* court failed to overrule *Roe v. Wade.* While coming up with several "reasons" why it wouldn't overrule *Roe v. Wade*, the court comes close to committing truth by almost admitting that *Griswold* and *Roe* were intentionally wrongly decided for political purposes in the first place.

The court then goes on to say that, although the facts[110]no longer support *Roe*, it would stick to its first answer and wouldn't overrule *Roe* because it would disappoint those groups, hasn't proved unworkable and also because to do so would damage the court's reputation [111]. The first and foremost question to consider is whether the decision is wrong – after all, we still do have a constitution in this country and the supreme court is supposed to follow it. The court's posture is like that of the best neurosurgeon in town who has a mortality rate of 90% for a delicate operation discovering a new and better technique that would allow 90% of his patients to survive, but then deciding not to use it because it wouldn't be fair to all his past patients who had died and that it would also harm his reputation if people were to question his consistency.[112]

Planned Parenthood v. Casey did show that the court, unlike Planned Parenthood, had by now definitely rejected the pixie dust argument

---

[110] Actually the medical facts known to all concerned never supported the decision in *Roe v. Wade* in the first place. However, *Roe* was an appeal from a hearing regarding declaratory relief and the denial of an injunction and so no medical testimony was even taken [odd since – even on a motion hearing – the only issue in the case was whether the right to remain alive attaches when life begins or at some future arbitrary time which may or may not be named later by the court]. To answer this question it was absolutely necessary that medical testimony be taken to establish that life indeed does begin at fertilization. This glaring defect allowed by the three federal judges in Texas played right into the supreme court's political penchant for creative writing and prestiverbitation.

[111] Would it even have been possible to further degrade the reputation of a court which had refused to follow the constitution, caved in repeatedly to political pressure, abandoned a neutral stance, violated the oaths of office of its members and flat out lied? If it were, only more of the same would be able to do it – truth and following the constitution could only be an improvement.

[112] Actually the supreme court's arguments are even worse because our hypothetical neurosurgeon just discovered the better technique whereas the supreme court has known all along that it is wrong.

as being too at odds with common sense and the medical facts to keep trying to sell to anyone. No coherent thesis is advanced by the court, however, as to why some "potential life" is more equal than other "potential life", especially since life itself begins at conception, but at least George Orwell would be proud. Other than those two relatively minor concessions, the supreme court's decision was a seemingly scholarly attempt to justify a position that was blatantly wrong on the facts and just as wrong on the constitution. Despite a disarming and seemingly scholarly discourse, the bottom line was that political cowardice ruled once again and the new rule of *stare decisis* became: If the court is wrong enough long enough ago, we can seem to be right as long as our wrong decision hasn't been 'unworkable 'and political considerations dictate that we continue to stick with our original wrong answer.

ACT V — A TALE OF TWO SENTENCES — WHERE THE ROAD TO PERDITION LED

In addition to inventing the constitutionally baseless right of marital privacy, the parallel bizarro bill of rights was also introduced by Goldberg in *Griswold v. Connecticut*. The court had no trouble in lying about what it had invented so as to spin it into the right of privacy on the magic loom of *Eisenstadt v. Baird*, and then enlarging it to include the right to kill a living human being[113] in *Roe v. Wade,* but faced a more vexing problem when it came to laying down rules of how a would-be right makes the journey from the bizarro bill of rights into the real one. The court's best guess as to how this might be accomplished was that when something is so fundamental that the forbidding the doing of it would be contrary to our country's system of justice, it is declared a fundamental, traditionally exercised and "deeply rooted" right Now a system of justice, as the name implies, consists of a series of procedural steps such as: arrest, preliminary examination, release

---

[113] Try as it might, not even the supreme court can deny that a preborn baby is a living human being.

on bond, pretrial motions, jury trial, etc., whereas a specific statute forbidding a certain activity – armed robbery, for example – is entirely substantive. Consequently it is impossible for a single substantive statute to be contrary to a whole series of procedural steps. You don't have to be a systems engineer or a high school graduate to figure this out, and so the supreme court was well aware of this distinction. As we have previously seen, few things stand in the way of a supposedly neutral and objective court reaching the goal it sets out to reach. The migration to the real bill of rights is even more awkward when you consider that the country did not even HAVE a system of justice when the bill of rights was adopted by congress in 1792, and so there was nothing for the targeted state laws to be contrary to.

In order for the favored new right to make this absolutely incredible journey out of nothingness and into the constitution so that any state law prohibiting the exercise of the newly favored fundamental 'right' moves the court to say that a state law prohibiting it would be contrary to the American system of justice, it must first be found to be "fundamental" or "deeply rooted". As awkward as this legal fiction was, it came to a screeching halt in the 2003 case of *Lawrence v. Texas*[114]. This was a case involving the conviction of two men of violating Texas' long standing law against sodomy. At the time of their conviction, sodomy was illegal in all 50 states (and at the time of decision was illegal in 49 states), had been illegal in all 13 original states and illegal in almost every country in the world 'til the memory of man runneth not to the contrary. This would seem to put the kibosh on the right to commit sodomy being deeply rooted. It was indeed, so the court simply sidestepped the issue and held that in the case of newly invented rights the term "newly emerging" could be substituted for "deeply rooted".

At this point the reader might suspect that I've finally gone too far and that no court would actually do such an outrageous thing, and so this must have been exaggerated rhetoric on the author's part to

---

[114] *Lawrence v. Texas*, 530 U.S. 558, 123 S. Ct. 2473, 56 L. ed. 2d 508(2003).

prove a point. Those readers are cordially invited to review the court's opinion itself, particularly the following language which appears at 323 S. Ct. 2484 and sounds like a progressive manifesto as the court wrote itself a blank check:

> "Had those who drew and ratified the Due Process Clauses of the Fifth Amendment or the Fourteenth Amendment known the components of liberty in its manifold possibilities, they might have been more specific. They did not presume to have this insight.[115] They knew times can blind us to certain truths[116]"

While neither the First Congress that adopted the Bill of Rights as the first ten amendments to the United States Constitution nor the 1866 Congress that adopted the fourteenth amendment most certainly did not know that "time can blind us to certain truths", the founding fathers did foresee that the constitution might need to be amended at some future date IF the democratically elected congress or state legislatures wanted to do that, since this is entirely consistent with the way republican forms of government are supposed to operate. If, however, the constitution were to be amended, such amendment would have to reflect the will of a two thirds majority of the people's democratically elected representatives, rather than just the will of the liberals, let alone five unelected liberal judges who have chosen to disregard the constitution as they've chosen sides in the culture wars. Article V of the constitution spells out exactly how this has to be done. Apparently these justices' oaths to uphold the constitution they were appointed to protect and defend against all domestic enemies don't

---

[115] How does the court know whether or not they "presumed to have" "this insight"? It's a pretty good bet, especially considering the history of the bill of rights, that the founding fathers 'presumed to have' all the insight they needed to have.

[116] No, they didn't. Imagine, if you will, James Madison presenting the bill of rights to the First Federal Congress whose powers would be significantly restrained by its passage, saying, "Of course, you understand that I don't presume to have the insight to know that there are probably going to be a lot more of these because you and I are blind to certain truths."

mean a whole lot to them. As Pogo said, "we have met the enemy and he is us."

The constitution has been amended twenty eight times, eighteen of those times having been since the bill of rights became part of the constitution in 1792: none of the amendments were the ones that the justices in *Roe, Eisenstadt, Casey,* Roe or *Lawrence* wanted, so they simply invented their own by torturous, prolix, internally inconsistent, politically inspired, yet supposedly neutral arguments and opinions. This explains the lack of logic, elastic standards which stretch to encompass whatever the court wants to encompass, deviousness and outright falsehoods which permeate the court's opinions in this area.

The court goes on to cite such overwhelming constitutional arguments as (1) although all 50 states had laws against sodomy in 1961, some state legislatures had repealed them [thus giving up the 'deeply rooted' idea and acknowledging that it is a legislative question in the same breath] (2) a tentative draft of the American Law Institute's Model Penal Code had recommended against state **legislatures** continuing to make sodomy a crime (3) the Illinois **legislature** had followed that recommendation (4) certain groups were in favor of state **legislatures** repealing their anti-sodomy laws and (5) a committee recommended that England's parliament repeal its law against sodomy which – after a mere ten year's study—it did, and then saved the Texas state legislature the trouble of repealing the law that it and certain groups didn't like and simply struck it down. Calling to mind the hierarchy of constitutional authority from a constitutional provision and a previous supreme court case on point being the highest to a graduation speech being the lowest as discussed earlier, we are now faced with a dizzying new array of supposed legal arguments so absurd that it's difficult to know where to start debunking them. Is it England's Parliament or the Illinois legislature which creates new constitutional rights? Perhaps neither of these has enough clout unless the American Law Institute Commission On Uniform State Laws <u>recommends</u> that state **legislatures** do or not do certain things.

The supreme court- itself one of the three branches of government— agrees with the United States Court of Appeals when it said in the 2005 case of *In Re WTC Disaster Site*[117] at page 466 of the Federal Reporter 3d. ". . . the federal government . . . cannot *require* the states to govern according to its instructions[emphasis by the court]. While chastising congress for again exceeding its powers in *Barenblatt v. United State*[118], the court noted that ALL THREE branches of the government have carefully delineated areas of concern, and that congress cannot meddle in matters that are exclusively the concern of the judiciary nor can it supplant the executive. *A fortiori*, then, the court cannot meddle in the matters which are purely legislative. It goes without saying, of course, that the Tenth Amendment of the constitution prevents any branch of the federal government from interfering with any state's internal affairs, including its penal code. U.S. Constitution, Amendment 10, American Jurisprudence 2d, Constitutional Law, section 236, p. 133, esp. footnotes 80 and 83.

The court now speaks in terms of "liberty interest" when deciding what new constitutional right it will invent next, and as we have just seen, has appointed itself as sole arbiter of what constitutes a liberty interest. Somehow the knowledge that the liberty interest basket didn't hadn't been invented until the court invented it 150 years later didn't faze the justices at all. What we have now – because of the supreme court's rewriting of the constitution to suit whatever ends it has in mind – is a new (and supposedly improved) fourteenth amendment that allows the supreme court to strike down whatever state law doesn't suit its fancy:

The real fourteenth amendment reads: " . . . nor shall any state deprive any person of life, liberty, or property without due process of law". Unfortunately, the fourteenth amendment as amended by the supreme court reads: ' . . . . nor shall any state deprive any person of life, liberty or property without due process of law **NOR OF ANY 'LIBERTY INTEREST' WITH OR WITHOUT DUE PROCESS OF LAW"**

---

[117] *In Re WTC Disaster Site*, 91 Fed 3d 466 (2nd circuit 2005). The supreme court case which was cited is *New York v. United States*, 505 U.S. 144, 122 S.Ct. 2408, 120 L. ed. 2d 120, on remand to 978 Fed 2d 705 (2nd circuit 1992)

[118] *Barenblatt v. United States*, 360 U.S. 113, 79 S. Ct. 40, 3 L Ed 1115 (1959)

This is by no means an exaggeration. Most liberal academicians and supreme court justices now accept as a given that the court should disregard the constitution at will and create new rights, with the only question being how and how soon the goal should be accomplished. For instance, in addressing the question raised by Justice Roberts in *Obergefel v. Hodges*, 576 U.S. _____, 135 S. Ct 2584, 192 L. Ed 2d 2609 (2015), "Just who do we think we are to redefine marriage", Harvard law professor Cass Sunstein took the main assumption for granted and castigated the court for waiting for a consensus to build before ignoring the constitution and creating a new right when he actually believes the court should be in the forefront of doing so.[119] We've descended a long way since Roscoe Pound came up with the doctrine of sociological jurisprudence. Even he thought the court should wait for the development of 'sociological facts' before deriving 'first principles' from them, whereas Professor Sunstein apparently thinks the court shouldn't wait, but should simply go ahead and derive whatever 'first principles' it wants to from its own enlightenment, the arc of history or moral commitments that he agrees with when the spirit moves them to disregard the constitution and strike down democratically enacted state laws. Imagine that: the most important moral question of the last half century is whether it is moral to even allow premeditated killing by abortion, and then along comes Professor Sunstein and says that condoning and encouraging such killings is the ONLY moral thing to do! Good grief, no wonder William F. Buckley said that he'd rather be governed by the first two thousand people in the Boston telephone directory than by the Harvard faculty.

It seems that even the court's staunchest defenders essentially plead guilty to what it stands accused of in this book, but contend that the court is nonetheless right as long as they agree with the political result. Professor Sunstein, for instance, thinks that the court should be a policy making body, should disregard the only legal way to amend the constitution (as set forth in Article V thereof), and simply amend

---

[119] *"Mr. Roberts, we are the People"*, article in the Bloomberg View as published in *The Kalamazoo Gazette* on July 30, 2015.

the constitution judicially by creating new 'rights' as the spirit moves it. He claims, however, that the court just doesn't make things up because when it does it has what it considers to be good reasons for doing so. These reasons include their own enlightenment, politics, popular opinion (decisions by poll watching) or how they view the "arc of history". To my knowledge, no one has ever accused that august body of randomly pulling new "rights" out of a hat for insertion into the constitution — that would be **randomly** making things up and inserting them into the constitution. His claim that since the court has reasons for making things up means that it doesn't actually make them up at all is nonsense. All it means is that such inventions are not random. The court hasn't sunk that far yet.

Ironically, the Declaration of Independence does contain a vague, ill defined and expandable phrase that would have provided the court some constitutional basis for its fanciful speculations if only it had been included in the bill of rights. The 'pursuit of happiness' was a concept separate from life and liberty. 'Liberty' meant freedom from imprisonment and confinement only and was not synonymous with 'the pursuit of happiness' or 'property', which is WHY it was intentionally left out of the bill of rights in the first place while life, property and liberty were included.

III

HOPE ON THE HORIZON OR JUST
ANOTHER POLITICIAN IN ROBES?

When Lana Kagan was nominated for a seat on the supreme court, constitutionalists and conservatives everywhere groaned. Wasn't this the liberal academic who barred military recruiters from the campus of Harvard Law School[120] and whose heroes themselves are activist judges? Since it was pure liberal politics that cast the deciding votes in the *Griswold, Eisenstadt v Baird., Roe v. Wade* and *Planned Parenthood v. Casey* cases, liberal politics that prevented the court from summoning up the strength and courage to overrule any of those four cases which it had intentionally wrongly decided and unabashed liberal politics that was responsible for what passed for legal reasoning in *Lawrence v. Texas*, weren't we just in for more of the same from yet another liberal supreme court justice? It would certainly seem so as there is nothing in her track record to suggest neutrality or a departure from the current supreme court majority which <u>continues</u> to let its politics interfere with its judging. The Senate Judiciary Committee was satisfied that she was lying and would continue to sacrifice the constitution to abet what has come to be euphemistically known as "abortion rights" when she

---

[120] As Justice Scalia points out in *Lawrence v. Texas*, the American Association of Law Schools had already banned any school that refuses to bar from its job-interview facilities a law firm (no matter how small) that does not wish to hire as a prospective partner a person who openly engages in homosexual conduct.

made the following amazing statement at her confirmation hearing:"
I cannot— I will not – let my politics interfere with my judging."[121]
Think about that – knowing full well that the only reason *Roe v. Wade*
hasn't yet been overruled is that the majority of justices on the court
did let – and continue to let – their liberal politics interfere with their
judging, along comes a justice who solemnly promises that, unlike
them, she will NOT let her politics interfere with her judging! The
only way that this can possibly happen is that Lana Kagan will vote to
overrule *Roe v. Wade* at her earliest opportunity.

It's only fair to give her a chance to prove herself. If her promise
goes unfulfilled – as her liberal and progressive defenders are counting
on — it will be far worse than just an unfulfilled promise: it will be
tantamount to fraud, because a promise made with no intention that
it will be carried out can be substituted for a misrepresentation of
fact in a fraud case.[122] While elevation to the nation's highest court all
too often has the effect of reducing nominees to the least common
denominator, it isn't always that way nor does it have to be that way.
Occasionally, a justice will realize that this isn't just a deceitful IQ
contest to be measured by who is the cleverest at getting around the
constitution, but rather that the worth of a supreme court justice is to
be measured by who lives up to the oath of office by upholding the
constitution and protecting it from all enemies, domestic and foreign.
There may be a proverb around that the damage wrought by one dean
of Harvard Law School can be corrected by another – if not, it's time
to start one.

There are those in this country who really do think that it is

---

[121] From Elena Kagan's opening statement to the Senate Judiciary Committee.
Had this statement actually been believed, her nomination wouldn't have been
consented to.

[122] *Hi-Way Motor Co. v. International Harvester Co.,* 398 Mich. 330; 247 NW2d 813
(1976): Michigan Civil Jury Instructions 128.03

far better for the emperor to lie about being naked than it is for a bystander to point out that he has no clothes As Ivan Denisovich said "one word of truth will outweigh the whole world."[123] He was right once – perhaps he can be right again.

---

[123] Alexander Solzhenitsyn, *One Day In The Life of Ivan Denisovich* Farrar, Straus, Giroux New York. Gillon Aitken, translator. 1971

GLOSSARY

ABORTION: The intentional killing of a living human being (sometimes called a fetus) prior to its birth.

BILL OF RIGHTS: The first ten amendments to the United States Constitution are known as the Bill of Rights. Not part of the original constitution, these amendments constitute restraints on congressional powers and feared overreach by the congress, and were insisted upon by the original thirteen states. After being culled from more than two hundred proposed recommendatory amendments submitted by the states, these few were enacted by the first congress four and a half years after the constitution was written.

COMMON LAW: As distinguished from law created by a legislative body or a written constitution, common law encompasses the body of those principles and rules of action which derive their authority from judgments and decrees of the courts recognizing, affirming and enforcing usages and customs from antiquity, particularly the unwritten law. The United States adopted English common law where not contrary to written statutes or constitutions.

CONSTITUTION OF THE UNITED STATES: The organic and fundamental governing document agreed upon by the people of the United States as the absolute rule of all departments and officers of the government in respect to all the points covered by it, which must control until changed by the authority which established it. Unlike the United States, England does not have a written constitution.

CONSTITUTIONAL AMENDMENT: A written change to the constitution which has been approved and adopted by two thirds of the Senate and two thirds of the House of Representatives. Amendments, which become part of the constitution when adopted, may also be proposed by a new constitutional convention.

CONCURRING SUPREME COURT OPINION: Written opinion by one or more justices of the supreme court wherein the justice(s) agree with the result reached by the majority of the court in a case, but for other or additional reasons.

DISSENTING OPINION: Written opinion by one or more of the supreme court justices wherein the dissenter(s) disagree with the result reached by the majority of the court in a case.

DUE PROCESS OF LAW: Law in its regular course of administration through courts of justice. It is a course of several legal procedures carried out regularly and in accordance with established rules and principles. Both the fifth and fourteenth amendments provide that no one shall be deprived of life, liberty or property without due process of law. Nothing in the constitution or any amendment thereto says anything about liberty interests.

EMANATION: Something that comes out of, or protrudes from, a source. As used by the court in *Griswold v. Connecticut*, the third amendment's prohibition on quartering troops in a person's house, the fourth amendment's protection against unreasonable searches and seizures, and the fifth amendment's allowing a criminal defendant not to testify against himself had emanations which, along with penumbras, gave rise to the new right of marital privacy. See Penumbra, *infra*.

FERTILIZATION: The process whereby human life begins by the male sperm penetrating the female ovum, chromosomes are exchanged when the two nuclei merge and a new human being is created which has the chromosomes of each parent, and then divides to become a blastocyst and then an embryo. This process takes about one second.

FIRST PRINCIPLES: In Harvard Law School Dean Roscoe Pound's view – and now in the supreme court's own view – these are the guidelines by which supreme court cases should be decided. These vague, subjective and ever changing 'first principles' cannot be derived from laws or the constitution, but rather only from vague, subjective and ever changing sociological facts. See sociological jurisprudence and social facts, *infra*.

GUARANTEE: The unfortunately named bill of rights is not actually a list of constitutional rights, but rather a list of restrictions and guarantees whereby congress is prevented from exceeding its narrow grant of legislative powers. If a law does exceed congress' power to have enacted it, it is unconstitutional for that reason.

HELPER RIGHT: A right, inserted into the constitution by the supreme court, which facilitates or makes more secure a right actually contained in the written constitution. Examples would be the right to sell and distribute newspapers, while not mentioned in the bill of rights, facilitates and makes more secure a right – freedom of the press—which actually is; the right to freedom of association, while not mentioned in the bill of rights, facilitates and makes more secure the right of freedom of assembly which is mentioned in the bill of rights. By the same token, freedom of thought makes more secure the right of free speech, and so on.

INHERENT: Existing in, and inseparable from, something else; involved in the constitution or essential character of something. Marital privacy is inherent in the marriage relationship as opposed to the supreme court's view that the fact that the women in *Griswold v. Connecticut* just happened to be married was coincidental, and so the newly invented right of individual privacy applies to unmarried people as well. When they got this one wrong, at least they did so intentionally.

LIBERTY: Freedom from physical restraint, or restraint on a person's ability to move about, such as freedom to travel or be free from arrest, imprisonment, being tied up or cast into a dungeon. Both the fifth and fourteenth amendment provide that no law shall be passed which deprives a person of life, liberty or property without due process of law.

LIBERTY INTEREST: An interest, recently invented by the supreme court, which includes those things which the court now thinks are fundamental interests and which no doubt would have been included in the bill of rights if only the states submitting the 200 recommendatoty amendments had had the foresight and insight to submit them to the first congress (and if the first congress had wished to be restrained far more than it grudgingly agreed to be). Neither the fifth nor the fourteenth amendments mention "liberty interest".

MARITAL PRIVACY: A phrase not found in the bill of rights, but coined by the supreme court because marriage is the cornerstone of western civilization and because constitutional prohibitions against quartering troops in people's houses, criminal defendants having to testify against themselves and unreasonable searches and seizures have emanations and penumbras which create the new right of marital privacy. Marital privacy, by definition, can only apply to married people. This changed when the supreme court later misrepresented its holding and claimed to have invented the right of individual privacy.

PENUMBRA: That part of a shadow which lies just outside the umbra (darkest part of the shadow). The supreme court said that constitutional prohibitions against quartering troops in people's houses, criminal defendants having to testify against themselves and against unreasonable searches and seizures have penumbras which, along with their emanations, create the right of marital privacy. See emanation, *supra*

PRIVACY (RIGHT OF): The supreme court said that the right of marital privacy really is the right of individual privacy, and was called marital privacy because the women in *Griswold v. Connecticut* just happened to be married.

PROCEDURAL LAW: That law which prescribes the method of enforcing rights or obtaining redress for their invasion. Contrast this with substantive law, *infra*.

QUICKENING: In medieval times it was believed that all the ingredients of life were present from the beginning of the pregnancy term, but did not jell or quicken into an actual life until approximately the 25th week of the pregnancy term. Now that we know that life itself begins at fertilization, the modern version of quickening holds that the mantle of personhood is not bestowed upon the living human being until approximately the 25th week of the pregnancy term. The rationale for this arbitrary time of bestowing the mantle of personhood is that that is when the baby is able to survive outside the womb.

SOCIAL FACTS: What Roscoe Pound thought – and what the supreme court today thinks – were and are the differing character, makeup, values and politics of society over a period of years. First principles, which are the criteria by which cases should be decided according to the doctrine of sociological jurisprudence, can only be derived from these vague, subjective and ever changing social facts. See first principles and sociological jurisprudence, *infra*.

SOCIOLOGICAL JURISPRUDENCE: This doctrine, proposed and championed by Harvard Law School Dean Roscoe Pound, holds that the supreme court should become a policy making body and decide cases based on what it deems to be first principles, rather than on the constitution. These vague, subjective and ever changing first principles cannot be derived from laws or the constitution, but only from vague, subjective and ever changing social facts. See first principles and social facts, *supra*.

SUBSTANCE: Essence; the material or essential part of a thing, as distinguished from 'form'.

SUBSTANTIVE LAW: That part of the law that creates, defines, and regulates rights, as opposed to procedural or remedial law which prescribes the method of enforcing the rights or obtaining redress for their invasion. See procedural law, *supra*.

Note: Definitions are from Blacks' Law Dictionary (fourth edition), Webster's New Collegiate Dictionary (seventh edition) and Dorland's Medical Dictionary (twenty sixth edition)

BIBLIOGRAPHY

BOOKS

A Fierce Discontent, The Rise and Fall of the Progressive Movement in America 1870-1920 Michael McGeer. Free Press, New York and London, 2003

Commentaries On The Law of England, Book the First, William Blackstone – Avalon Project of The Yale Law School

Context of The Bill of Rights, Stephen Schecter and Richard Bernstein, editors. New York Commission on the Bicentennial of the United States Constitution, Albany, New York 1990

English Constitutional History, Thomas Pitt Taswell-Langmead, eleventh edition. Theodore F.T. Plunckett, LLB, MA, LLD London 1960

Hegel in 90 Minutes, Paul Strathern, Ivan R. Dee, Inc. Chicago 1977

In Quest of Freedom, Alpheus Thomas Mason and Richard H. Leach, Prentice-Hall, Inc.., Englewood Cliffs, New Jersey 1959

Life In The Making, Alan Frank Guttmacher, Garden City Publishing, Inc. Garden City, New Jersey and New York 1933

Miracle At Philadelphia, Catherine Drinker Bowen, Little, Brown and Company Boston, New York and London 1969

One Day In The Life Of Ivan Denisovich, Alexander Solzhenitsyn, Gillin Aitken, translator, Farrar, Straus, Giroux 1971

Search and Seizure, Wayne La Fave, Thompson-Reuters Publishing Co. Minneapolis 2004

The Bill Of Rights, Government Proscribed, Ronald Hoffman and Peter J. Albert, editors University of Virginia Press for The Unites States Historical Society, Charlottesville and London 1997

The Heritage Guide To The Constitution, Edwin Meese III, David F. Forte and Matthew Spalding, editors, The Heritage Foundation Washington, D.C. 2005

The Justices of the United States Supreme Court, Leon Friedman and Fred L. Israel, Chelses House Publishers, New York and London 1969

The Virginia State Constitution, A Reference Guide, John Dinan, C. Alan Tarr, series editor Westport, Connecticut and London 2003

PERIODICALS -

A Man's Home Was Not His Castle: Origins of The Fourth Amendment, C. William Cuddihy and B. Carmon Hardy, The William and Mary Quarterly 3rd series, Vol. 37, No. 3 (1980)

Book Review: Roscoe Pound and Carl Llewellyn: Searching For An American Jurisprudence, N.E.H. Hull. The Cambridge Law Journal, Vol. 58 No. 1 (1999)

Colonial Writs of Assistance, Emily Hickman, New England Quarterly Vol. 5, No. 1 (1932)

Origins of the Fourth Amendment, Leonard W. Levy, Political Science Quarterly, Vol. 114, No. 1 (Spring 1999)

Recovering The Fourth Amendment, Thomas Y. Davis Vol. 98, Michigan Law Review No. 3 (December 1999)

The Right To Be Let Alone, Commencement Address by Erwin Griswold appearing in Northwestern University Law Review Vol. 55 at pp 216 *et seq.* (1961)

DOCUMENTS -

A Declaration By The Representatives of the United Colonies of North America Now Met in Congress At Philadelphia Setting Forth The Causes And Necessity of Their Taking Up Arms [1776] Avalon Project of The Yale Law School

[English] Bill of Rights, 1689

Constitution of Connecticut, 1776 Avalon Project of The Yale Law School

Constitution of Georgia. 1776 Avalon Project of The Yale Law School

Constitution of Maryland, 1776 Avalon Project of The Yale Law School

Constitution of the Commonwealth of Massachusetts, 1776

Constitution of New Hampshire, 1776 Avalon Project of The Yale Law School

Constitution of New Jersey, 1776 Avalon Project of The Yale Law School

Constitution of New York, 1776 Avalon Project of The Yale Law School

Constitution of North Carolina, 1776 Avalon Project of The Yale Law School

Constitution of Pennsylvania, 1776

Constitution of Rhode Island, 1776

Constitution of South Carolina, 1776 Avalon Project of The Yale Law School

Constitution of The United States as Amended by the First Foederal Congress, 1792

Constitution of Virginia, 1776

Declaration of Independence, 1776

Declaration And Resolves of The First Continental Congress, 1774 Avalon Project of The Yale Law School

Declaration Of The Rights Of Man, 1789 [French]

Draft of The Constitution of The United States [with the original Article Four crossed out by the draftsman]. On display at the National Archives.

Magna Carta, 1215

Ratification of The Constitution By The State of Rhode Island, 1790 Avalon Project of The Yale Law School

Texas Penal Code, sections 19.02 and 19.03

The Federalist Papers (esp. Federalist No. 84), National Home Library Foundation, Sherman Miller, editor

Virginia Declaration of Rights, 1776 Avalon Project of The Yale Law School

NEWSPAPER ARTICLES

Before Knocking Judicial Activism, Think About Privacy. Article by Carol Towarnicky of The Philadelphia Dailey News, Appearing in The Detroit Free Press on August 24, 2005

Doh! What's The Bill of Rights? Article by The Associated Press regarding a survey taken by the McCormick Tribune Freedom Museum appearing in the Detroit News on March 1, 2006

Mr. Roberts, We Are The People. Article by Harvard Law School Professor Cass Sunstein in the Bloomberg View as published in the Kalamazoo Gazette on June 30, 2015.

What Did Lincoln Do? Article by Eli Savit, appearing in The Detroit Free Press on September 28, 2011

APPENDIX 1

THE BILL OF RIGHTS, BEING THE FIRST TEN AMENDMENTS TO THE UNITED STATES CONSTITUTION AS ACCEPTED BY THE FIRST FOEDERAL CONGRESS IN 1792

AMENDMENT I

Congress shall make no law respecting an establishment of religion, or prohibiting the free exercise thereof; or abridging, the freedom of speech, or of the press, or of the right of people peaceably to assemble, and to petition the Government for a redress of grievances.

AMENDMENT II

A well regulated Militia, being necessary to the security of a free State, the right of the people to keep and bear Arms shall not be infringed.

AMENDMENT III

No soldier shall, in time of peace be quartered in any house, without the Consent of the Owner, nor in time of war, but in a manner to be prescribed by law.

AMENDMENT IV

The right of the people to be secure in their persons, houses, papers, and effects, against unreasonable searches and seizures, shall not be violated, and no Warrants shall issue, but upon probable cause, supported by Oath or affirmation, and particularly describing the place to be searched, and the persons or things to be seized.

AMENDMENT V

No person shall be held to answer for a capital, or otherwise infamous crime, unless on a presentment or indictment of a Grand Jury, except in cases arising in the land or naval forces, or in the Militia, when in actual service in time of War or public danger; nor shall any person be subject for the same offence to be twice put in jeopardy of life or limb, nor shall be compelled, in any criminal case, to be a witness against himself, nor to be deprived of life or liberty without due process of law, nor shall private property be taken for public use just compensation.

AMENDMENT VI

In all criminal prosecutions, the accused shall enjoy the right to a speedy and public trial, by an impartial jury of the State and district wherein the crime shall have been committed; which district shall previously been ascertained by law, and to be informed of the nature and cause of the accusation; to be confronted with the witnesses against him; to have compulsory process for obtaining witnesses in his favor, and to have the assistance of counsel for his defence.

AMENDMENT VII

In Suits at common law, where the value in controversy shall exceed twenty dollars, the right of trial by jury shall be preserved, and no fact tried to a jury shall be otherwise re- examined in any Court of the United States than according to the rules of the common law.

AMENDMENT VIII

Excessive bail shall not be required, nor excessive fines imposed, nor cruel and unusual punishment be inflicted.

AMENDMENT IX

The enumeration in the Constitution of certain rights shall not be construed to deny or disparage others retained by the people.

AMENDMENT X

The powers not delegated to the United States by the Constitution, nor prohibited to it by the States, are reserved to the states respectively, or to the people.

APPENDIX 2

THE REAL FOURTEENTH AMENDMENT

NO STATE SHALL MAKE OR ENFORCE ANY LAW WHICH SHALL ABRIDGE THE PRIVILEGES OR IMMUNITIES OF CITIZENS OF THE UNITED STATES; NOR SHALL ANY STATE DEPRIVE ANY PERSON OF LIFE, LIBERTY OR PROPERTY WITHOUT DUE PROCESS OF LAW

[NOTE THAT NOTHING IS SAID HERE [OR ANYWHERE ELSE IN THE CONSTITUTION] ABOUT PROHIBITING THE DEPRIVATION OF "LIBERTY INTEREST" WITH OR WITHOUT DUE PROCESS OF LAW].

APPENDIX 3

ARTICLE V OF THE CONSTITUTION

THE CONGRESS, WHENEVER TWO THIRDS OF BOTH HOUSES SHALL DEEM IT NECESSARY, SHALL PROPOSE AMENDMENTS TO THIS CONSTITUTION, OR, ON THE APPLICATION OF THE LEGISLATURES OF TWO THIRDS OF THE SEVERAL STATES, SHALL CALL A CONVENTION FOR PROPOSING AMENDMENTS, WHICH, IN EITHER CASE, SHALL BE VALID FOR ALL INTENTS AND PURPOSES, AS PART OF THIS CONSTITUTION, WHEN RATIFIED BY THE LEGISLATURES OF THREE FOURTHS OF THE SEVERAL STATES, OR BY THE CONVENTIONS IN THREE FOURTHS OF THE SEVERAL STATES, OR BY THE CONVENTIONS IN THREE FOURTHS THEREOF, AS ONE OR THE OTHER MODE OF RATIFICATION MAY BE PROPOSED BY CONGRESS . . .

NOTE; THE MANNER OF AMENDING THE CONSTITUTION IS EXCLUSIVE. THERE IS NO PROVISION ALLOWING THE SUPREME COURT TO INVENT NEW RIGHTS AND THEN STRIKE DOWN DEMOCRATICALLY ENACTED STATE LAWS WHICH DO NOT CONFORM TO THESE HERETOFORE NON-EXISTANT NEW RIGHTS]

INDEX

Judicial doubletalk 64, 90

L

Law review article 50, 54
Least common denominator 101
Liberty interest 60, 97, 104, 106, 119
Little person 79

M

Mason, George 11, 29, 36, 40

N

Nineteenth Amendment 71
Non logical thinking 64

O

Orwell, George 93
Outdated laws 21

P

Penumbras 42, 43, 45, 55, 88, 104, 106
Planned Parenthood v. Casey 83, 87, 92, 100
Point shaving prosecutor 27
Political cowardice 91, 93
Probable cause 14, 35, 36, 43, 45, 46, 48, 116
Progressive 4, 5, 6, 7, 84, 95, 101, 109
Pushed man 83
Pythagoreans 20, 81, 82

Q

Quartering of troops 18, 45

R

Roscoe Pound 4, 6, 7, 84, 98, 105, 107, 110

S

Schopenhauer 27
Search warrants 14, 18, 36, 43, 45, 47
Slam dunk for the baby 86
Social engineering 6
Social facts 5, 105, 107
Sociological Jurisprudence ix, 5, 98, 105, 107

T

Tail Gunner Joe 51
Tautology 66
Time can blind us to certain truths 95

U

Unknow a fact 81

W

Weighing and balancing 84, 85, 86
Wet spaghetti approach 42, 59, 87
Wilkes and Liberty 15
Wilson, Woodrow 4, 6, 84